Nathen,

Thanks so much for your support & friendship all this while. Your association has made a huge positive impact on my life. Look forward to life long friendship...

Pursue Legendary,

Himanshu
Nair

LEGENDARY
CONSULTING

HOW TO CONSULT LIKE THE
Top 1%

HIMANSHU NARANG

BEX

Legendary Consulting. How to Consult Like the Top 1%
Himanshu Narang

PUBLISHED BY BEX

Print book ISBN 10: 1-68411-519-1
Print book ISBN 13: 978-1-68411-519-8

Subject: Consulting Skills

Copyright © 2018 Himanshu Narang

All rights reserved. No part of this publication may be reproduced, stored in a retrieval system, or transmitted in any form or by any means, electronic, mechanical, recording or otherwise, without the prior written permission of the author.

Interior design by Mariana Vidakovics De Victor

"It is not the critic who counts: not the man who points out how the strong man stumbles, or where the doer of deeds could have done them better. The credit belongs to the man who is actually in the arena, whose face is marred by dust and sweat and blood....who at best knows, in the end, the triumph of high achievement, and who at the worst, if fails, at least fails while daring greatly...."

- THEODORE ROOSEVELT

Dedication

To my parents and grandparents for their love and teachings that drive me forward and keep me grounded every single day.

And to my beautiful wife and best friend, Meenal, for being the rock-solid pillar of support, she is to me.

Contents

Preface 11
Acknowledgements 13
Introduction 15
« Chapter One » Legendary Consulting 23
   What Makes Consulting Challenging 26
   Thirteen Traits of Legendary Consultants 30
   The Seven Mindsets of a Legendary Consultant 36
« Chapter Two » Personal Mastery 43
   Understanding Yourself 44
   Understanding Productivity 50
   Managing Stress 63
   Rocket Fueling Your Growth with a Mentor 68
      Benefits of Having a Mentor 69
      How to Find a Mentor? 71
« Chapter Three » Proposal Mastery 77
   The Three Types of Proposals 79
   Right Attitude for Proposal Writing 82
   What Makes the Difference 87
« Chapter Four » Relationship and Positioning Mastery 101
   Key Practices for Effective Relationship Building
   and Positioning 102
« Chapter Five » Communication Skills Mastery 123
   One-on-one Business Conversations 126
      Bullet Point Speaking Framework 127
      Body Language 132

>   Listening 136
>   Giving Feedback 139
> Presentation Skills and Speaking.....................................142
>   Structure 144
>   PowerPoint 148
>   Delivery...150
> Leading Effective Meetings 154
> Email and Phone Communication 160
>   Pros and Cons of Different Communication Media........ 160
>   Which Communication Medium Should You Choose? .163
>   Strategies for Effective Email Communication..................164
>   Strategies for Effective Phone Communication................ 167
> Communicating Technical Information
> to Non-Technical People.. 172
> « Chapter Six » Leadership Mastery..................................... 179
> Prerequisites to Effective Leadership 182
> Key Practices and Strategies for Effective Leadership 185
> Handling Client Objections...192
> Leadership with Difficult People.......................................196
> « Chapter Seven » Quality Mastery 203
> Five Pillars of Quality..204
> Seven Strategies for Quality Improvement..........................208
> Conclusion and Next Steps..223
> Readings...229

Preface

This book to me is an expression of my desire to be a contribution and make an impact. It is an expression of my core values and principles. I strongly believe that excellence in consulting is a gift to the society and to the world.

In this book, I have distilled some of the most cutting-edge concepts and tactics in the realm of consulting effectiveness. These are concepts and tactics that I strongly believe have the power to positively transform your consulting results in the shortest time.

Even though I have diversified and expanded into Corporate Training and Professional Speaking since starting out as a Consultant, I still consult and consulting is and will remain my first love. The thrill of engaging in a new project with a brand new set of people, to solve a business problem or to tap into an opportunity is second to none. I love the adrenaline rush that comes from facing challenges, dealing with resistance and overcoming the odds to deliver a high-quality result.

Although the consulting services industry has grown to over $500B globally, excluding the revenue from internal consulting teams, I found that there were not enough consulting skills focused books in the market that would cover the entire scope of what it takes to be an effective consultant. This is the book which I would have paid a fortune to read if it existed when I was starting out.

The process of bringing this book to life was long, complex and full of learning and reflection. It took over two years of focused work, but I believe this was the most professionally rewarding phase of my life. I met and gathered insights from consultants from different parts of the world. I have grown a lot as a Consultant and Trainer in the process of compiling this content and presenting it in the most easily understandable manner.

The journey was also full of doubt and disbelief. It went from struggling to accept the fact that I could be an author, to feeling scared of putting my work out there for the world to see and judge. I had to consistently tell myself it is going to be all right and that people would love it and benefit from it. And here I am. It is in front of you now.

I am grateful for the opportunity to serve you.

Acknowledgements

This book has become a reality due to the teaching, mentorship, coaching, friendship and support of many individuals. I would like to take this opportunity to thank all of them.

Foremost, I would like to extend my thanks to my parents for growing me up and building into me the courage, the wisdom, and the skill set required to write this book.

Many teachers, mentors, colleagues, friends and family members have influenced me positively, shaped my thinking and contributed to the manifestation of this book. Some of them are:

My mentors that have always shown me the right path: Yurik Sandino, Abelardo Mayoral, Roger Killen and Gobinder Gill

Leaders that have enabled my growth: Eduardo Garza, Ken Catlabuga and Grant Candy

Colleagues that have supported me: Karen Reutlinger and Robin Suprun

Consulting leaders that provided me insights from their experiences: John Ray, Arun Sharma, Mohammad Asif, Raymond Jones, Steve Lee, Tina Fan, Michael Browler, Martha Jenning, Tony Ding, Swati Bhardwaj, Karen Lasdek and Phillip Upton

My fellow Toastmasters that have always cheered me on: Keith Gillingham, James Dean Waryk, David Lee, Raj Thobhani, Wendy Chernoff, Casper Shyr and Jules Kulea

My teachers that impacted me through their wisdom and

insight: Blake Hanna, Darren Dahl , Phil Arrata and Murali Chandrashekaran

People that believed in me even when I did not: Mark Rowlands, Cheryl-Dean Thompson, George Harjani, Dustin Hogan and Ryan Zokol

And my best friends that have supported me unconditionally: Pav Bajwa, Rahul Shah, Nathen Aswell, Anubhav Sachdeva, Sanjeev Puri, Damanpreet Singh and Argelio Santos.

Finally, and most importantly, I would like to thank my wife, Meenal, who spent countless hours with me reviewing and finalizing the content, the design, the launch and everything in between. Meenal complements all my weaknesses and has made a huge impact on this book through her knowledge and intelligence.

Thank you all for your friendship and guidance in the tough times and in the good times.

Himanshu Narang
New Westminster, British Columbia
14th January, 2018

Introduction

"He was not a practical joke nor was he a fool, but he was determinedly original and had a vague and modest idea of himself as a legendary figure."
- JOHN CHEEVER, THE SWIMMER

Congratulations on picking this book up on the legendary consulting system. More importantly, congratulations for beginning your journey to improving yourself as a consultant – aspiring to consult like the top one percent. The mere fact that you've picked this book up is evidence that you're someone who is committed to growth, improvement and creating greatness through results in whatever you do.

I'll start off by sharing a personal story from my early life. I still remember it like it was yesterday: I was fourteen years old and driving in India with my parents in our cherry red Maruti Suzuki 800cc. It was winter, and the streets were veiled in fog. As we drove along, I was selecting subjects for my next school year. At that time in India, you chose a track – medical, commerce, arts, etc. – and I was trying to decide which one to choose. We were discussing this as we drove and I asked my father, "Dad, what should I choose so that I can lead a successful, fulfilling and rich life?" Even though I was young, I already knew that I wanted to be really successful in my life. At that age, I probably didn't even fully understand the concept of success, but I'd heard people around me discuss this idea. From listening to them, I'd learned that success was something to which I should aspire.

When I asked my dad this question, about what I should do to be successful, his answer was something that completely changed my view of the world. It transformed my perspective on everything I did from that time onward. And, indeed, his answer that day continues to drive my life even now: influencing everything I do. What he said was this: "Son, being successful, being fulfilled, being enriched, it's not about what you do; it's about being good at what you do." My fourteen-year-old head exploded: Wow! This one little statement completely transformed my view of the world in a single moment. And that impact continues to this very day: it's not about what you do, but how good you are at what you do.

Propelled by my dad's nugget of wisdom that winter day, driving along in the cherry red Maruti Suzuki 800, I have been inspired to immerse myself in the science of human effectiveness: what makes humans effective? What distinguishes the ultra-performers from the also-rans? What differentiates those who produce breakthrough results from everyone else in the world?

As it happened, like a good Indian kid, I eventually chose to become an engineer. I started working as an internal consultant to a manufacturing company. I was fortunate to work with some of the world's leading professionals in business strategy and process improvement. I then moved on to do my Masters in Business Administration at the University of British Columbia. Upon graduation from UBC, I undertook consulting work in the healthcare industry focused on operations strategy and business process improvement.

Since then, over the last few years, I've had the opportunity to deliver business strategy and operations improvement

Introduction

focused consulting in all major industries, including information technology, food and beverage, energy, education services, transportation, etc.

Through all these experiences, working with a wide range of business professionals, I came to recognize specific patterns from observing those who produced excellent results, made a difference in their clients' lives, in their business and in the world. I also noticed that consultants who were good at what they did, adding value to their clients' lives and businesses, were consistently more fulfilled in their own lives. They were happier and more excited about their lives, who they were and what they were doing for others. As my father suggested all those years ago, it turned out indeed that being good at what we do is a necessity for feeling fulfilled in our lives. Being good at what we do gives us the satisfaction of making a difference.

So, the lesson that I'd invite you to take away from this story is that being a legendary consultant not only requires striving for greatness in your career, it entails attention to every aspect of your life. Such an aspiration affects us intellectually, physically, financially, socially and spiritually. Being legendary in your consulting work will transform your life in more ways than you can imagine.

Consulting is both science and art. It blends a diverse and broad set of skills. In contrast to so many other professions, it is an opportunity to express our real selves. Of course, every profession has its pros and cons; each adds some value to the world. But consulting, I believe, is unique in the range of opportunities it provides us to express ourselves; to make the maximum use of the full set of skills in our toolbox and to achieve our fullest potential.

On any given day, a consultant uses multiple skills: analytical, interpersonal, technical, communication, time management, project management, presentation, selling and planning skills. All of these skills converge to create an effective consultant. That is what makes consulting such a fascinating and thrilling career. The ultimate consultants are those who can analytically pursue solutions to their central core; who build great relationships; who communicate complex ideas with pure clarity; and efficiently juggle multiple ideas, projects, and clients. That's why I say that consulting is such an exciting mix of science and art that uniquely allows us to express our fullest potential.

And, surely, one of the highest human needs is to achieve our utmost potential. Unlived potential, unrealized dreams, unused skills, are the source of terrible regret. Consulting offers us a remarkable opportunity for personal fulfillment. Simultaneously though, it also provides us the opportunity to add value to the lives of others. In helping others solve their problems, we are able to play a significant role in contributing to the improvement of their businesses and lives. Even Tony Robbins claims contribution and significance are core human needs (T. Robbins, 2014).

All of these lessons I have learned from the experience of working with over 250 consultants during the last several years. I've had the opportunity to lead and contribute to projects with a total budget of over $1 billion. I've had the chance to be trained, mentored and coached by some of the most extraordinary consultants in the world. My aptitude for observing patterns has identified what distinguishes the great consultants from the rest. Everything I've learned from all this experience, from business, education, training courses and observing other consultants, I will distill for you into easily accessible chapters that open the door of my own insights, knowledge, and experience. The lessons you will learn here will enable you to achieve optimum effectiveness in your consulting efforts, right from day one, providing you the tools, the skills and the strategies to begin your path toward legendary consulting.

As a part of my research to finalize the content of this book, I also ran surveys and interviewed 75 of the best consultants in the world that I could get access to. The information I gathered from all of this research was structured around one question only – What is it that differentiates the Top 1% Consultants from everyone else? The insights I received from those extraordinary consulting brains have been spread across the book and will be available for you to use and benefit from starting today.

I always say the law of cause and effect applies to every situation. What do I mean by this? For every effect, there is a cause – a reason. If you can find the reason, you can duplicate the result. For example, if you wanted to make butter chicken, it would be helpful if you had a butter chicken recipe. If following that recipe provides you butter chicken, once, next time, if you follow the same formula, you can rely upon duplicating the results of the same butter chicken. Similarly, there is a recipe for being a great and legendary consultant. There is a recipe for consulting like the top one percent. This recipe I call the legendary consulting system. Following this recipe, you can achieve those results. Following the legendary consulting system, you will gain the skills and outlook that lifts the world's greatest consultants to the top of their game.

This book is laid out in seven chapters. The first chapter is called Legendary Consulting. That's where I'll explain what legendary consulting is and explore the measures by which we judge such legendary achievement. Plus, we'll look at some of the challenges that consultants face in their day to day lives and the mindset that legendary consultants employ to overcome those challenges.

Following that introduction to legendary consulting, the ideas discussed in the rest of the book will be organized into six different mastery areas. These are the areas you need to master to be able to consult like the top one percent. Combined, these are what I call the legendary consulting system. The first of these six areas I call Personal Mastery. As the old saying goes, you have to change yourself before you can presume to change the world. What do we need to get right about ourselves before we can help others? The second mastery area is Proposal Mastery. This is the art of writing and delivering master proposal documents and presentations: proposals that get to "yes." I have extensive experience in guiding and mentoring people who are pitching ideas to prospective clients. I'll share all this with you. Area three is Relationship and Positioning Mastery. At its essence, consulting is a relationship business; it's about dealing with people. Consulting success depends upon your ability to position yourself successfully: as your clients' trusted adviser; as a partner; as somebody with whom they would want to associate with. How you can do that is explored in this fourth chapter.

Chapter five emphasizes Communication Mastery. Communication is the canvas that binds the world. Here we'll explore improving your communication skills: in a one-to-one setting, in a one-to-many setting, in public speaking, email, or over the phone. How do the top one percent manage these communication scenarios? We'll explore what distinguishes them and how you too can achieve excellent communication skills. You'll learn how to read body language, how to be assertive, polite, give feedback and make a recommendation. These are vital skills for great consulting.

In chapter six, we'll explore Leadership Mastery. Here we learn how to deal with different kinds of clients, including those who show resistance. For instance, do you know how to walk a client through the solution development process? This is a vitally important ability, and I'll show you how the world's top consultants do it. You'll learn how to deal with objections and differences of opinion; ask the right questions and look beneath the surface of appearances; manage expectations; and, most pressing of all, identify what is most important to your clients.

In the final mastery area, we'll explore Quality. Consultants make up to $5000 an hour. Why would clients pay so much for their advice? This is because of the market advantage that comes from superior quality. Consultants bring specialized problem-solving skills and a robust understanding of the best practices in the field. These are benefits which permanent employees are not always able to provide. Besides this, Consultants deliver high-quality work that makes an impact on the client's business. I have found that quality is a result of getting things right. If you get things right, the quality follows. In this final chapter, we'll look at different ideas, strategies and planning frameworks available to improve the quality of your own outputs. Again, these are lessons you'll be able to apply starting right from day one.

In the end, we'll review all the mastery areas and wind up with a broad overview of how to achieve excellence as a consultant. Once you've mastered these six areas, you will be a legendary consultant and the path to personal fulfillment and outstanding success will open before you.

I would invite you to understand that the skills, strategies, and tactics you will have access to in this book apply to all types of consulting roles. In fact, I can guarantee any form of customer-facing professional including investment bankers, coaches, customer service representatives, trainers, network marketers, financial services representatives, etc. will benefit from it.

I'm excited to be your guide and friend in this journey to legendary consulting success. I'm confident that once you've put in the time and effort to master these areas, skills, and perspectives, you will become a legendary consultant. You will add value to your clients' lives. You will help them transform their businesses. And, in the process, as my father taught me all those years ago, driving through the fog in that cherry red Maruti Suzuki on an Indian winter day, you'll discover that being great at what you do is also the path to your own success, fulfillment and personal enrichment.

I'm excited to take this journey with you through the legendary consulting system. Are you? Well, then, let's dive in.

« CHAPTER ONE »

Legendary Consulting

*"Don't wish it was easier,
Wish you were better.
Don't wish for less problems,
Wish for more skills.
Don't wish for less challenge,
Wish for more wisdom."*

- JIM ROHN

In this chapter, we will discuss the nature of legendary consulting and its objectives.

Legendary consulting is the ability to add tangible value effortlessly. It requires an approach to consulting that is genuine, ethical, honest, and effective. Being a part of the top one percent in consulting, in the end, starts with being a good human being. That's a general goal towards which we all should aspire, but its importance perhaps applies to consulting more than any other profession. As we go through the legendary consulting system, exploring the skills and challenges of being a great consultant, we'll return time and again to the central importance of this idea of being a genuine and ethical person.

Legendary consulting is not just about providing the best analysis, conducting the best presentation, building the best relationships, or even the timely completion of work. Yes, it is of course about all these things, but it is above all about adding tangible value in the most effortless way possible. When a legendary consultant is involved, everything looks easy.

However, you must remember that it is not the client's responsibility to extract value from your consulting efforts; it is your responsibility as a consultant to deliver that value to your clients. Let me repeat that because this insight is the game changer. Recognizing this fact and its importance is what I've discovered to be one of the factors that separate the top one percent of consultants from everyone else. Adding value to the client's life is the responsibility of the consultant. Aside from the ethical responsibility we have as consultants to ensure those hiring us are not being shortchanged on their investments in us, this is an eminently practical concern. The truth is that sometimes our clients are not even sure what it is that they need. From the client's perspective, the problem might merely be something like this: "We're not making enough money," "We have too many expenses," "Our customer attrition rate is too high," "Customer satisfaction is too low," "We're not retaining our best employees," "Our server downtime is too long," or even that their health is suffering from their business' stress.

Such clients are experiencing a problem which is harmful to their business and life, but cannot put their finger on the root cause that requires change. Knowing that one needs a solution in no way ensures that one knows what that solution would be, nor even where it is needed. Consider an example of a client who is troubled by the fact that their business is not making enough money. They want to increase their profitability, but what is the underlying problem? They don't know. Are their operational costs too high? Are they out of sync with the market? Are they spending too much money on marketing, sales, systems or finance? Are fixed costs too high? All they're sure of is that the bottom line is not working out as expected or required. What's to be done? This is where the job of the consultant comes into play. Your goal is to get the information needed, to ask probing questions, and perform the analyses which allow you to get to the heart of the problem. Only by correcting the root cause of the client's revenue problem will they experience a lasting solution that meets their needs.

Achieving these results is not easy; sometimes the discovery process involved in getting at these root causes do not prove possible over a single conversation. It is sometimes necessary for you to have several conversations before you discover what's underlying the apparent problem. Sometimes it can take months of analysis to unearth the root cause of the business' problems. It can be a long and challenging process to not merely address the client's complaint but identifying the source of that complaint – the cause, which once corrected, solves the problem not just for today but for the future. That's a centrally important part of the job of the legendary consultant.

So, it's not enough to merely follow the clients in the direction they want to go, you must steer them in the direction they *need* to go – even if they don't yet know it. That is how you provide them real value. This is a crucial part of the consultant's job, bringing into play many diverse and essential skills. This is what makes consulting such an exciting sport – so to speak. And it's this side of it that excites me so much about the work and life of being a consultant.

What Makes Consulting Challenging

This is a good point to address the challenges of consulting. What makes it difficult to be an effective consultant? Understanding this will help us, as we move into the mastery areas that follow, to recognize what we are trying to mitigate and toward what ends we are trying to build solutions.

1. A leading challenge to effective consulting is the requirement of *dealing with all different kinds of people*. Consulting work requires dealing with a diverse range of possible personalities on a consistent basis. The consultant could be working with one, to several, to dozens, to even hundreds of clients per year. That is challenging. Every client you meet is bringing to your discussions a different set of skills, beliefs, values, and fears. An effective consulting practice needs to cater to every single one of these distinct individuals. Consulting is a high-value service, and any high-value service must be tailored to the unique needs of the client. Undoubtedly, different clients can enter initial conversations with a consultant possessing a wide range of expectations. Some of these are more realistic than others. Always though, it is the job of a consultant to ensure that, going forward, we work from the same playbook as the client.

    Personally, in the past, I've experienced challenges in achieving this end. There have been times I've not been able to successfully manage expectations or build the required rapport. There have been times when I've been unable to position myself in the necessary way. Consulting is a relationship-building business, and not all personalities lend themselves to good, long-term relationships. All clients will be different. This is a reality of the job. It is a reality though, that can be mitigated with the right skills and attitudes.

Also, as the world has become more interconnected, we now have business environments in cities all over the globe where all kinds of people from different backgrounds are trying to work together. Geographic distances though are much more easily and quickly crossed than cultural ones. When we move around the world, we tend to bring our cultural differences with us. The result can be some friction in the grating of very different expectations and values. For example, those from Asian countries, such as China and India, are not inclined to make eye contact, especially when dealing with someone who is a work-superior and especially someone they respect. In North America though, failure to make eye contact can be a taken as a sign of disrespect, lack of confidence and possibly dishonesty. Awareness of such cultural diversity, and how to cope with it, can be the difference between a failed or successful consulting effort.

2. Another challenge is the consultant's need to be able to *understand the client's world*, from the outside, in a short time span. As consultants, your job is to enter the client's world to solve a problem. Your ability to provide that solution depends upon your ability to understand the client's world. The client, of course, has had an entire lifetime or career to build this world and become immersed in it. You, on the other hand, have a very short window of opportunity to absorb all this information. This requires a vigorous strategy with minimum input. You have time to ask

some questions; read some reports; study their financial statements, marketing plans, etc. All this must be done efficiently, in a short time span.

3. A third challenge to the consultant is that the *perception of the quality of delivered consulting services is subjective*. This is something we'll return to at length in chapter seven. It means that you and the client may not always see eye-to-eye in your perceptions. As a consultant, you may do everything right, yet the client may fail to perceive what you've actually contributed. Understanding clients and their expectations is a central challenge. Some clients want to build a more personal relationship with the consultant while others only want to talk business. If you go into a meeting with the latter type of client asking how their children are doing or what they did over the weekend, the gesture won't be appreciated. To those clients, this behavior can seem intrusive and even rude. Yet, there are also clients to whom, if you enter the room immediately talking bottom lines and leveraging resources, you'll seem cold and impersonal. This is an example of the art side of consulting. Being able to study and understand people is necessary. You have to be able to read who they are and what added value they're looking for from you.

4. A fourth challenge to consulting is that you often find yourself in the apparently ironic situation of *coaching the expert*. The leader of the company or unit is in that position for a reason. They are likely an authority in the industry and certainly the expert on their own company or team. Yet, you've been brought in to coach them on how to get more out of

their organization. Definitely, if the company has brought in a consultant, you can expect the leader to be open to listening and learning, but neither the leader nor you can ignore who the expert is, on this particular business. That situation is a tricky one that requires tremendous attention to and ability in communication skills. Employing your communication skills to position yourself as a trusted adviser becomes critical. Choosing the right language to pose your recommendations is imperative. Egos come into play. Even the experts, put in the situation of having to learn from an outsider, can become defensive. After all, the very need to bring in a consultant can be interpreted as an adverse judgment on the expert's priorities and past performance. Wouldn't you feel a little sensitive in that situation?

5. *Personal drivers* are another challenge to effective consulting. Sometimes people are primarily driven by different priorities and concerns. For instance, a manager may choose a strategy based upon their own personal incentives. If you come in as the consultant, recognizing that another approach would be better, the manager may push back against your recommendations, not from the grounding of a sound business perspective, but by this personal commitment to the original strategy. Identifying where such drivers are at work and understanding how to handle them is another challenging aspect of the consultant's job.

6. *Expectations of the client* can be a real challenge for the consultant, too. Some clients expect you to come in like some kind of a wizard, with a magic wand, able to immediately wave away all their difficulties and problems. You want to

do well for your clients, and you want them to expect this of us. However, unrealistic expectations are damaging to everyone involved. Managing such unrealistic expectations is an important challenge for achieving effective consulting.

7. Finally, among the variety of challenges for effective consulting, a major one is the *diverse skill set that is required by a consultant*. This theme is one already mentioned above, and that will be explored in greater depth as we proceed, but it's important to keep in mind while taking an inventory of the challenges posed to effective consulting. There is a vast range of skills a consultant needs. And while not every one of them is used every single day, they are continually being called upon to deal with the everyday challenges of the job. It is precisely the necessity both to be aware of this need and manage it in the best way possible, that inspired me to write this book. My objective has been to bring together the essential catalog of such skills into one convenient place for your easy access.

Thirteen Traits of Legendary Consultants

I have identified thirteen traits which distinguish legendary consultants from all the rest. These are the qualities that propel the best consultants into the top one percent. So it is critical that we identify and appreciate the nature and significance of these traits.

1. The first of the thirteen traits is *clarity of vision*. Great consultants are able to see the end clearly from the very be-

ginning of the project. Right from the start, they make a specific effort to craft their vision of the project. When someone knows their goal, and in what direction they're heading, the followers emerge. Knowing your vision from the start allows you to effectively communicate it throughout the project. This clarity of vision and communication helps the clients and support teams to come aboard with confidence and purpose. This is vital for the successful delivery of the service.

2. The second trait of legendary consultant is *strong observation skills*. Great consultants can get beneath the surface appearance of things and recognize revealing facts about the situation which are not evident to everyone. An essential aspect of this trait is the ability to sense discomfort in the mind of the client. Furthermore, it is important to be able to identify the causes of that discomfort. What isn't working? How are the client's efforts falling short of their aspirations? And why is that happening? Uncovering all this is essential to successful consulting, and requires tremendous observational skills.

3. The third trait is a *belief in their own ability*. Confidence is a game changer. When you believe in something, it shows. I often say that consulting is a lot like sales: every day we are selling our ideas, recommendations, beliefs, experience, and vision. Having confidence and conviction in our experience, ability, and vision makes all the difference in selling others on our contributions. This is where the idea of effortlessness comes into play. When you genuinely believe in yourself, your training, experience, ability, and vi-

sion, selling clients on the value, you'll bring to their lives, and business is effortless.

4. Legendary consultants are also *clear and concise communicators*. They can respond to complex questions with answers that are clear and precise. Those who do not possess this trait are always in danger of wandering off into unknown territories. None of us should be disconcerted by this prospect. The ability to provide a clear, crisp, concise answer to even the most challenging questions is a learnable skill that we will explore later in this book.

5. Trait number five is *strength in relationship building*. Legendary consultants excel at relationship building. In no other field is the skin-in-the-game more rooted in the relationships you build. It is an intensely human experience, requiring you to confront many emotions as you deal with a wide range of values, beliefs, and experiences. We, humans, are incredibly social animals and this aspect of our nature comes to the fore in coaching and partnering – central traits of successful consulting. This relationship building though is not achieved through bland compromise and trying to blend in with the crowd. On the contrary, the legendary consultant achieves relationship building success by bringing a unique authenticity to the table. Being authentic not only distinguishes you as an exclusive individual, but it is also the foundation of a sincere and honest relationship, which will cultivate trust.

6. *Strong analytical skills* are the sixth trait of the legendary consultant. Those with this trait are great analysts, who can get to the root cause and identify the best solution using a

solid empirical base: wading through the data and asking revealing questions. Furthermore, they do this in a timely manner. They are not merely effective, they are efficient. This analytical ability comes with training, experience, and openness to learning.

7. The seventh trait of legendary consultants is *robust planning*. This is another of those dimensions of the legendary consulting system that will be reiterated time and again throughout this book. Robust planning allows you to vastly optimize all your other abilities across multiple platforms. Consultants with great planning skills can work with numerous clients, tackle various projects, and coordinate with multiple teams. Furthermore, they are able to do this precisely when they are most challenged: in turbulent and uncertain times when complexity is high, and the outcome path is unclear. Doing that takes exceptional planning.

8. The legendary consultants' eighth trait is the *capacity to influence*. This is their ability to win buy-in from all those involved in a project: the client, client's team and any other collaborators or stakeholders. Success only comes if everyone's thought process is aligned. Otherwise, energies are wasted and time is squandered. For this beneficial situation to be achieved, the consultant's ability to influence others to buy into their vision is essential. The top one percent of consultants have developed this ability.

9. The ninth trait of the legendary consultant is exceptional *listening skills*. This is another trait that is reiterated throughout the book. Listening requires being patient and focused. This trait is especially important to emphasize as

it can be too easily misunderstood. After all, we all listen all the time. What can be the difficulty? Active listening though, aimed at solution searching, is another thing. It is a skill that needs to be cultivated. And the research shows it is a necessary component of business success. As my mom used to say, the person listening is the one in charge of the conversation. They know what questions need to be asked next, and are in the position to decide the most fruitful direction of the discussion.

10. An *addiction to intense focus* is the tenth trait of the legendary consultant. Distraction kills creativity. It takes ninety minutes of concentration to tap into our inner genius. This is what is called the flow state of our brain. Science has shown that tapping into this flow is how we open up green fields of creativity (Csikszentmihalyi, 2008). This is how we deliver our most outstanding and profound results. So focus is essential to success, and the great consultants are able to demonstrate this. I have observed that the very best, the top one percent, have this extraordinary capacity to focus on the challenge at hand.

11. The eleventh trait of legendary consultants is that they are *self-starters*. They are self-motivated. They don't need a push from the client or a teammate. Although the term self-starter has become something of an industry cliché these days, we must not let that cloud our appreciation of how important it is to successful consulting. This trait is especially compelling when unexpected challenges arise in a project. It is all too easy, under such circumstances, to look for a little mental break. This may not necessarily be a bad

thing, but it can too easily slide into procrastination. The legendary consultant does not hesitate under such conditions to confront the new challenge head-on.

12. The legendary consultants' twelfth trait is *responsibility*. They don't blame others, and they don't make excuses. The truth is that nobody has it all together all the time. The grass is always greener somewhere else. No team has all the training. No infrastructure provides all the support. No consultant has all the answers. And no client has everything you want them to be able to contribute. Given that reality, when things aren't going as well as you'd like, it's so easy to lapse into the blame game: to come up with a long list of excuses for inadequate performance. If you want to consult like the top one percent though, there can be no blaming on others or making excuses. The legendary consultant takes responsibility. The legendary consultant acts as the last line of defense.

13. The thirteenth, and final trait of legendary consultants is their *strength of leadership*. They can bring people together, build a cohesive team and steer them toward a common goal. They unite clients, teammates, support staff, fellow consultants and everyone involved, behind a shared vision. They can stir the excitement for the pursuit of a common cause. Having everyone rowing together, in the same direction, is essential to project success. The legendary consultant's leadership is instrumental in making this happen.

The Seven Mindsets of a Legendary Consultant

Having the right mindset in the game is central to success in any walk of life. If you don't have your mindset right, your reflexive responses will be suboptimal. As we'll see, there are some particularly challenging aspects of having the correct mindset for a successful consultant. In this section, we review the seven mindsets that, once achieved, will enable you to be a legendary consultant.

1. *Value addition and contribution* is the first of the seven mindsets needed to be a legendary consultant. Great consultants are focused on making a difference in their clients' business. This is what drives them. This is why they come to work every day. This fact implies that such people would not pursue work where they believe they could not add value. This is a core characteristic of the legendary consultant, and I'd invite you to wire this temperament into your brain.

2. The second mindset of the legendary consultant is an emphasis on *working today for a better tomorrow*. This involves front-loading the work. The overwhelming majority of the great consultants I've had the opportunity to work with and observe have had an uncanny ability for getting the bulk of the work set up or done in the first week of the project. From the very start, they set the tone and scope of the job. This is working today for a better tomorrow. Working this way establishes a positive attitude around the project right from the start. The team is excited. The client is thrilled. This quickness out of the gate is a result of for-

ward-thinking: chalking out a plan, a strategy, and a vision. The result is a powerful and shared sense of optimism that fuels everyone.

3. *An evidence focus* is the third mindset of the legendary consultant. The top one percent of consultants are distinguished by the fact that they do not make assumptions. They test everything out. They look for the evidence, be that in the raw data or secondary research findings. They don't allow their own personal biases to come into the office with them. They aspire to be as open to the evidence as possible. Unchecked preconceived notions about appropriate solutions can send the most well-intended consulting exercise into a tailspin that serves nobody's interests: not the client's, not the team's, and not even the consultant's. Definitely, you can learn, from past experience, lessons which may be helpful in a future consulting challenge, but the legendary consultant never tries to get by with plug-and-play solution strategies. Not every problem is a protruding nail; the consultant can't walk into a project always armed with only the same old hammer.

4. The fourth mindset of the legendary consultant is a *commitment to ethics*. This was briefly discussed above; let's accentuate it, here. The importance of this commitment cannot be overstated. I assume the fact that you're reading this book indicates that you're serious about consulting as a long-term career. If that's true, hear this and don't forget it, please: success is going to rely on your reputation. Maybe not exclusively, but inevitably. Let's say that a good reputation is not sufficient – but is undoubtedly a necessary

condition for successful and legendary consulting. Maintaining a reputation for high standards is as important a selling feature of your consulting service as there is. And this should not be confused with pandering to the client. There are many lures into unethical traps. Sometimes clients, or their representatives, want you to support solutions which are not the most logical or ethical approach. Such people may be involved in their own internal power struggles, trying to influence superiors, directors, shareholders, etc. Endorsing misleading conclusions to aid in these processes reduces you to a puppet in their game. This is not a proper performance of your duty of care. Falling into these traps, placating clients in the short term, will cost you your reputation as a good steward, in the long run. Only strong ethical standards and a commitment to stand by those standards, even when it's difficult, can show you the right path.

5. This understanding of the importance of ethical commitment, even when that requires rejecting the expectations of some clients, leads us directly into the fifth mindset of the legendary consultant: *challenging the status quo*. In the world of business, which is usually quite hierarchical, with chains of command, and everyone answering to someone, this might seem like a dubious mindset to have as a consultant. Upon closer reflection, this isn't as strange as it may seem at first glance. After all, if what was being done was working, they wouldn't likely be bringing in a consultant, would they? No, but I know rubberstamping approvals brings consulting firms some business. That is not what we are discussing here because that can lead to unethical consulting.

We are talking about strategies on how to build a long-term successful and impactful consulting career.

So, by its very nature, consulting is about looking for a different way of doing things. This requires you to maintain a high-level of curiosity; be critical of what exists; look for innovative approaches; challenge assumptions and test suggestions. Innovation virtually is a result of having challenged the status quo. You can't add value to your client's life and business if you merely replicate the same little box within which they've been thinking all along. It is precisely because of the difficulty we all have in getting outside of our own little thought boxes that your client has brought you in – for a fresh perspective. You were hired to think outside of the box. The box is the status quo, and your job is to get outside of it. One has to let go of what one already has to be able to open the door to what can potentially exist. Our job as legendary consultants is to help our clients make that transition.

6. The sixth mindset of the legendary consultant is one that for most people is by definition uncomfortable: *finding comfort in discomfort*. The great consultants are wired for this in a way that is uncommon. When the situation is so complicated, when the chaos of the situation is so overwhelming, when uncertainty confronts every next move, when most people want to curl up and hide away from the onslaught of such emotional discomfort and cognitive overload, this is when the legendary consultant rises to the occasion and raises their game. This is a game-changing mindset. Consultants are constantly inundated with uncomfortable cir-

cumstances: meeting new people, absorbing fresh information, facing new problems, working in new environments and cultures, with new institutional constraints and expectations. This is not how most people do their job. At its core, consulting entails situations of discomfort that most people rarely ever encounter. Success as a consultant then requires learning how to find a comfort zone within this daily experience of discomfort. Ultimately, there is a transition to a world where discomfort becomes the new normal. For the legendary consultant, discomfort becomes the new comfort.

7. Finally, *forever student* is the seventh mindset of the legendary consultant. Legendary consultants are always looking to learn: to grow, expand, and diversify. They are fascinated by information and have managed to turn that fascination into success. They are enticed by expertise and want to learn from the experts. They want to read books. They are excited at the opportunity of training courses. They take online courses. They attend seminars. There's no end to what they want to learn. Such people never rest on their laurels in their education or knowledge. They are forever students. This is not an easy thing to be. Opening one's self up to learning leaves one in a vulnerable state. When you ask someone to teach you something, you're acknowledging a shortcoming, even a weakness. Too many people miss great learning opportunities because bravado protects them from that vulnerability. The price of such false security though is the loss of an opportunity to gain authentic confidence through growth and learning.

1 - Legendary Consulting

The fact that you're reading this book demonstrates that you are not one of those closed off by the need for false security, but instead are in earnest pursuit of genuine confidence, based on real knowledge. Reading this book tells us that you are on the path to being a forever student: committed to learning new things and becoming a master of your craft. That's what legendary consulting comes down to, willingness to invest the time and effort to make yourself a master of consulting. Whether that be learning new skills, refining those you have or cultivating the mindsets necessary to excel, the legendary consulting system is an uncompromising pursuit of greatness. So, congratulations to you for reading this book and forging your own path toward becoming one of the top one percent of consultants.

With this fundamental understanding of what it is to be and aspire to be a legendary consultant sketched out in this chapter, we're now in a position to look in more detail at the precise skills you will need to become a great consultant. Besides the mastery areas, one of the core ideas at the heart of this book that I would like you to embrace is continuous improvement. Developing the six mastery areas and working on traits and mindsets of a legendary consultant, will enable you to get better every day: showing up tomorrow stronger than you are today.

The world is consistently changing; an expert today will not be one tomorrow. Technologies, markets, customers, data, so many things that make up our work environment, are in a constant state of flux. Consequently, all kinds of new strategies, tools, and research methods have emerged. Staying competitive requires us to keep on the cutting-edge of these innovations. The next six chapters will be a great help to you in this mission to continuously learn and improve your attitudes, skills, and tools.

« CHAPTER TWO »
Personal Mastery

*"Knowing others is intelligence
Knowing yourself is true wisdom
Mastering others is strength
Mastering yourself is true power."*
- LAO TZU

There is immense power that comes from mastering yourself and the forces that press upon you. Mastering the factors that allow you to perform at your peak will enable you to make a difference in the world. This mastery involves self-management and self-discipline. How effective we are at what we do, and the impact we have in the world all depends on our capacity for this self-management and self-discipline. Performance expert Harris Kern characterizes this as the motor that drives our lives (Kern, 2014). Personal mastery is about understanding ourselves: clear-eyed belief of who we are and an honest evaluation of our performance. This requires understanding the forces that affect us and mastering our interaction with them. This involves recognizing the factors that determine our performance: be it mediocre, above average, excellent or legendary.

Legendary consulting starts with mastering yourself, understanding what drives your performance, knowing what makes you productive and fulfilled. Leveraging these insights is the primary condition for achieving the status of a legendary consultant. This chapter breaks our discussion of the topic into four main components: the first is understanding yourself, the second is understanding productivity, the third is managing stress and, the fourth component is rocket fueling your growth with a mentor.

Understanding Yourself

Understanding who you are is the initial step in the all-important process of discovering your purpose. Your purpose is your motivation: the answer to why you do what you do. This may sound esoteric or even triumphant. This is not limited to some exclusive circle of geniuses and heroes. We all have a purpose, an aspiration or vision that animates us, wakes us up in the morning and makes us stand back up every time we're knocked down. This is what it is to be human. However, there is a difference between merely being blindly led by one's purpose and consciously acknowledging and embracing one's purpose.

That is where we'll start: **understanding why you are a consultant**. What do you like about it and what value do you want to add to your life by consulting? For some people, it might be the opportunity to make a difference in the lives of others. To others, it might be the opportunity to make new friends and establish new contacts. Some might be excited by the challenges of working to solve new business problems. For still others consulting might be seen as the best means to continually grow as a person and professional. And for yet others, it might be the opportunity to create wealth or travel the world. Any of these or numerous others could be what motivates you: provides your purpose for taking on the life of a consultant. You need to start by discovering your own purpose. This purpose will fuel you forward and make you productive.

Let's figure it out here. Why did you become a consultant? Or, why do you want to become a consultant? There are no wrong answers to this question. Think. Think about your why. Think beyond yourself. Think about what impact you want to make on the world.

YOUR PURPOSE

_____

_____

_____

_____

_____

_____

The second step of self-understanding is **defining your vision**. It is difficult to hit a target you cannot see! You need to explicitly set your long-term goal. Where do you see yourself in five years? Fifteen years? Twenty? The legendary consultants, those who add the most value to their clients' lives and businesses, are those who know their own direction. Having a clear sense of direction is essential for making the right choices about the work you want to do, the clients you want to work with. Knowing your direction is the key to discovering your path. Knowing your path is necessary for identifying what you need to do to follow that path. Direction clarifies choices. Clarity fuels mastery. Mastery is the mother of good work. The top one percent of consultants achieve their success and status because they have this clear vision of their direction.

You need to be sure that you're clear about your vision. In this component, I invite you to identify your vision: where do you see yourself? What type of a job do you want? What kind of business do you want to have? What kind of clients do you want to work with as your consulting business matures? How many clients do you want? What services do you want to deliver? Where do you want to live and work? The country and the city you're in now or do you see yourself somewhere else? And when you've accomplished all that, how will you feel? What will you see? What will you experience? This is what I mean by vision. When you can, in your mind's eye, see what your life would be like once you've followed your own path, then we can say you've defined your vision.

Describe your five, ten and twenty year vision now.

YOUR VISION

_____

_____

_____

_____

Understanding your core values is the critical third step in self-mastery. Your core values are what drive you. These are the privileged preferences that inform your life. They establish your priorities and serve as a measure of success, judged in your own terms. These are the guideposts that help you decide what to do when you come to one of life's many forks in the road. Which way do you go? What choice do you make? A sound grasp of your core values is the key that unlocks these mysteries and challenges. They enable you to make a choice, and indeed the right choice, for your life. If you know your core values and can rely on them when making your decisions along the path of life, you will be able to look back and feel confident that life's challenges never led you astray, never diverted you from your path.

What are we considering under this rubric of core values? Here are some possibilities you might want to consider: achievement, relationships, financial independence, ethics, commitment, compassion, health, professional growth, excellence, mastery, trust, security, freedom, contribution, impact, etc. Whatever drives you; whatever animates you; whatever gives you a sense of meaning, these are your core values.

Personally, my single most important core value is building relationships. If I neglect the key relationships in my life, I'm left unhappy, I don't feel fulfilled. That's my first core value. My second is excellence, being the best at what I do. Otherwise, I do not feel at ease and that I'm living a good life. And my third core value is impact. A desire to have a positive impact on our society and the world. I want to make a difference and contribute. That is what excites me about my life. Understanding all this, recognizing the centrality of these core values to my life took time and effort, reflection and self-interrogation. Making the time and putting in the effort has been of incalculable benefit in allowing me to understand how I want to live my life and pursue my consulting career.

Identifying your top three core values will be equally as important for your life and career. I invite you to identify your top three core values. What are they? Reflect on that and identify them below.

Your Core Values

_____

_____

_____

_____

_____

Understanding your SWOT is the last component of understanding yourself. SWOT is an acronym for Strengths, Weaknesses, Opportunities, and Threats. This refers to having a robust understanding of your skills set and your personality. Having this understanding enables you to drive your work in the right direction, position your services efficiently, attract ideal clients and build a thriving consulting practice.

So, how do you go about using this tool to understand yourself? The first two parts: Strengths and Weaknesses are internal to you. These will be based on your skill set and your personality. For example communication skills, attention to detail, analytical skills, interpersonal skills, etc. The second two parts: Opportunities and Threats are external to you. These are based on macro factors like market trends, economy, consumer behavior, etc. that can impact your work. Understanding your opportunities and threats from external sources is critical in today's business environment where things are changing at a faster pace than ever before.

So, let's perform a SWOT analysis on yourself below:

Your SWOT Analysis

Strengths	**Weaknesses**
Opportunities	**Threats**

In summary, understanding yourself is about, first, finding your purpose: why do you do what you do, and more importantly, why are you in consulting? What are you trying to achieve? Second, it is about defining your vision: where do you see yourself down the road? What is your dream? The third key of self-understanding is discovering your core values: what are the top three priorities that drive you? The fourth key is about understanding your SWOT. I implore you to explore all three of these dimensions thoroughly, before moving on to the next component.

Understanding Productivity

The second component in personal mastery is understanding productivity. Productivity is widely overlooked in our society, today. There is indeed a vague sense that it's essential. People have a general appreciation that they can do better. From my experience though, most of us do not pay nearly sufficient attention to it. This is an opportunity to entirely distinguish yourself from almost everyone else; in your practice, on your team, and in your industry. High-level productivity enriches your own life too, as Chris Bailey demonstrates in *The Productivity Project* (Bailey, 2016). Understand what makes you productive; what enables you to produce better results more efficiently.

Before you can understand your own productivity, let's be clear about what productivity is precisely. Let's try to define it. Undoubtedly, productivity can mean different things to different people. I interpret it as your velocity toward your goal. Don't confuse this with simple-minded ideas of quantity. Being able to respond to 20 emails in an hour doesn't necessarily make you productive. It may only mean you're fast. If your job is answering email, that would be productive. Otherwise, it just tells us a small part of the story. Productivity is about channeling your energy toward tasks that most require your attention: tasks that get you closer to your deliverables. Attending to those tasks is what makes you productive.

For the productive consultant or anyone in any walk of life, the steps that get you closer to your goal are the productive ones. Whether that end goal is a service, a strategy, or a material object: delivering it is the definition of being productive. So productivity is defined by taking steps to get us there. The more we concentrate on the effective steps, the sooner we'll get to our goals. To reiterate, productivity is your velocity toward your goal.

I'm going to share with you some cutting edge productivity strategies that I use and have learned from leading consultants around the world. Let's start with setting up a perspective that will put these ideas into context.

I moved to Canada, from India, in 2012, with no network and limited English fluency. Not knowing anyone in Vancouver, as you could imagine, I faced many challenges. I struggled to connect with people, to make friends, to even feel hopeful. In the summer of 2013, when I had to find an internship, you can appreciate the challenge this posed. I submitted hundreds of applications before being accepted into one at a factory in Delta, British Columbia. For those of you who don't know the geography of the British Columbian lower mainland, this entailed a daily commute of 1.5 to 2 hours in each direction from where I lived. Things were a bit difficult. Plus, I knew that there were past graduates from my program who were still unable to find work in the consulting field. So, yes, things did look bleak.

In December 2013, after completing my MBA program at University of British Columbia, I returned to India to visit my family. While I was there, I had a discussion with my mother about my future prospects in Canada. I told her how difficult things were, just as I've told you. She replied in a way that caused my thinking to take a 360 degrees turn. She said, son, I know it's going to be difficult; sometimes you cannot control the results. Sometimes the outcomes are not exclusively in your hands. All you need to do, and all you can do, is make today count. Just focus on what needs to be done today. That's all you can control. If you need to apply for any jobs, apply today; if you need to send any emails, send them today; whatever you need to do, do it today. Then, tomorrow, do what needs to be done tomorrow. Don't worry about the results; they will take care of themselves. Just make today count.

Evidently, this isn't rocket science. It is a simple idea. But, too often this simple insight is what we overlook: the importance of getting things done, now. The significance of the present day: making today count. Everything I share with you about the importance of productivity is geared to help you make your days COUNT. To make this advice easier to remember, I've structured the principles for better productivity around the acronym COUNT.

Cheerful Associations: As Jim Rohn said: "You are the average of the five people you spend the most time with." The people you associate with impact your life, your thoughts, and your ideas. Your choice of who to spend your time with therefore impacts your work performance. Keeping away from toxic people is vital. You know: these are people who are always complaining. These are people who have a problem for every solution: people who drain you emotionally. Sometimes, in other cases, people just don't jibe with who you are; you don't share a mutual perspective or value system. My invitation to you is to stay away from such people as much as you possibly can.

I understand this is easier said than done. Instead, try to cultivate cheerful associations: people who cheer you on and make you feel inspired and happy. If you spend most of your time with people you find uplifting, you will feel elevated in your aspirations. As a consultant, you want to add value to the lives of others, but why shouldn't you have value added to your life? If you strive for cheerful associations, your relationship with others will add value to your life. Achieving such associations has a considerable impact on your performance. Jim Rohn's statement that you are the average of the five people you spend your time with has come to be regarded as a bit of a cliché. The principle of cheerful association though, emphasizes the core truth of this claim. It's such a simple, yet amazingly effective means of improving your life quality. Yet, it is something too many of us often neglect.

I had initially met one of my best friends, Ryan, at a local Toastmasters Club chapter back at the beginning of 2016. We decided to meet, one-on-one, over a coffee. In that first meeting, we chatted for over two hours. I don't remember what exactly we discussed. What I do remember is how Ryan made me feel. He made me feel like a million dollars. We all have the need to be appreciated and valued by others. That was my engaging experience of this meeting with Ryan. Over the subsequent period, we've stayed in touch, collaborated on multiple projects and are in the process of co-authoring a book. My association with Ryan has had a hugely positive effect on my life. Just that one cheerful association has changed my life and will continue to do so in the future.

Who are you spending your time with? Someone that inspires you? That makes you a better person? Of course, it's difficult to eliminate those who share a long history with you. If those people though, are a drain on your life; if they make you unhappy or discouraged, being successful requires you do it or at least maintain a distance. This is a difficult decision that every successful person has had to make; it is an action that every successful person has had to take. The sooner you can do it, the better off you will be. Be conscious of your associations and honest about who deserves your time, attention and energy. Strive for cheerful association.

Who are the people you want to spend more or less time with? Identify them below. If you want to associate with new professionals from the industry, create a plan to connect with them. You might meet them through LinkedIn, Industry conferences, Association meetings, Events, Meetup groups, etc. What's your plan?

YOUR CHEERFUL ASSOCIATION PLAN

_____

_____

_____

_____

_____

Olympian Planning: Plan your days like the best of the best. I did forewarn you that planning would be a constantly reiterated theme of this book. I've had the pleasure and good fortune of working with and training some of today's most successful business people. From this experience, I cannot fail to notice that one of the factors that differentiate them from everyone else is how they plan their day. For instance, how do you start your day? How you start your day sets the tone for how you'll live that day. Now you might ask, what is the most effective start of the day? Science suggests that even a quick workout at the beginning of the day makes a massive difference to the rest of your day (Hillman, Erickson, & Kramer, 2008; Tomporowski, 2003). You don't necessarily need to hit a gym. You might have a resistance training routine you can do in your backyard, or you can take a jog around the block. You want to get your heart rate up, build a sweat, and release endorphins. This will raise your energy level and make you feel good. That sets a great tone for the rest of the day. Research also shows that people who start their day with a workout experience less fatigue and procrastination (Fahmy, 2008; Pozen, 2001).

Another vital aspect of Olympian planning for the day is the time at which you start your day. When do you start yours? There is massive alignment between successful people and when they start their day (Lubin & Gillett, 2016). Eighty-five percent of Fortune 500 companies' CEOs start their day before 6 a.m. Some of them start as early as 3:30. They call it a head start for a reason! If you were running a race for all the marbles, wouldn't you like a head start? That's exactly what you're getting when you rise early to begin your day. Get going, say, with that workout, before the emails start rolling in, before the phone starts ringing, before the text messages start alerting your phone. These people all usually start three hours before everyone else. Sometimes, with the quietness and focus, early morning allows you to get your whole day's work done by noon. I usually start my day at 5:30 – sometimes even earlier. Often, by 10:00 am, I find myself having completed more than most people accomplish in their entire day. As should be obvious, then, that is a huge productivity hack that you can integrate into your life. Yes, it is difficult. It takes time. It's a pain at first, but persistence will win the day. Research tells us that it takes 66 days to install a new habit (UCL, 2009). So, if you can manage to get yourself up early every day, for just over two months, you'll find it getting easier and easier until finally, it's effortless. The advantages you'll reap will be enormous.

The third aspect of Olympian planning is Pre-Game Preparation. This takes only 15 minutes, ideally after your workout and shower, where you craft your to-do list with your top 5 action items for the day. These are outcomes if accomplished would make your day a successful day. This 15-minute practice is powerful. It set the tone for a legendary day and most of the ultra-performers I know engage in this on a consistent basis. So, how you begin your day sets the flow for how you live your day. How you live your day defines your performance. And your performance is the key to your productivity in business, consulting, and indeed in everything you do and achieve in your lifetime.

This leads us into the fourth aspect of Olympian planning, how you measure your performance. How do you know you've lived a good, productive day? My approach here has been derived from the lean management approach. I break my day down into three categories. Each of my 24 hours in the day is allocated to each of three categories. First, is customer value-added. This is the work that translates into dollars. This is something for which my customers are willing to pay. Something like data analysis would fit this category. Second is business value added. These are activities that customers may not want to purchase, but they are necessary for my business to stay and grow in the future. Strange as it first may sound, an example of this category would be sleep. Just because I want you to rise early doesn't mean I want you to be sleep deprived. You can't be effective and productive if you are. Good sleep is important for being productive, but your customers aren't going to pay you for it. Cooking, eating, hygiene, exercise, all these necessary activities fall into this category of business value added. Besides these, my investments in personal and professional growth also fall in this category. The third category is non-value added time. Surfing the internet or watching escapist television is an example of this. These activities may provide pleasure and possibly even valuable downtime, but they do not add value to either my customers or my business.

When considering how you allocate your time, think of your choices in terms of these three categories. It will help you identify your daily activities and be more conscious of the implications of your choices. Are they your best choices? Are they your most productive choices? You may discover that you're not doing your customers or your business the best that you could in your allocation of time. Thinking of your day this way helps you become aware of your choices and your options. This opens the door to improved productivity.

How do you recharge yourself? Are you sleeping enough? I've just mentioned the importance of getting enough sleep. Most people need seven to eight hours to function at peak performance levels for a sustained period of time. Do you get out into nature, breathe some fresh air, and get away from texts and emails? How about taking some time off from work every few months: a little sabbatical. Do you eat well? Do you eat good quality food? You should be reducing your calorie intake toward the end of the day. It promotes better sleep and general improvement in your health.

This is Olympian Planning, getting the plan for your day right, so you can optimize your productivity. Create your own daily plan below. What do you do to start your day? Do you begin with a work out? What time do you start your day? Do you begin your day with a head start? Are you engaging in the pre-game preparation? How do you measure your performance over the course of a day? Are you conscious of where the value added is in your choices? And how do you recharge yourself? Do you eat and sleep well and take time to clear your head? Consider the best practices described above.

Your Daily Plan

_____

_____

_____

_____

_____

Undefeatable Happiness: The next letter in our COUNT acronym points to a heavyweight pillar in productivity. Plenty of research has confirmed that those who are genuinely happy are more productive, close more sales, make more money, are more likely to be promoted, live longer and are more likely to make new friends (Sgroi, 2015). There's no doubt about the powerful link between happiness and productivity. The question is, how does one achieve happiness? We tend to think of happiness as something that happens to us. We go about our business in the world, and things either go well, or they don't. If they do, we're happy; if not, we're unhappy.

This way of thinking though has a fundamental error at its heart. According to Robert A. Emmons, Professor of Psychology at the University of California, Davis, there are practices you can follow that actually make you happier (Emmons, 2008). You can cultivate synaptic pathways in your brain that generate the same experience associated with externally generated happiness. Let's consider some of the practices that you can use to train your mind for experiencing happiness.

Gratitude is a reaction we can prime ourselves for, deliberately, through a conscious focus on the things for which we're grateful. This gratitude generates happiness. We all have so much to be grateful for. It's just a matter of being open to appreciating those things.

Another practice that really works for me is visualization. Visualizing our goals and dreams allows us to see ourselves living the life we want. Mary Ann Troiani, the co-author of *Spontaneous Optimism (Troiani & Mercer, 1998),* says that if you experience that visualization with your eyes closed, your mind doesn't know if it's real or unreal. Neuropsychological pathways make the experience feel real, tricking your mind into thinking what you've visualized is real. This increases confidence in the experience. Visualization can be done efficiently in a few minutes each day. I think of this as reconnecting with my dreams. This forecasting of an optimum future can trigger the happiness responses in your brain.

What daily practices are you going to adopt to improve your happiness quotient? What time would you practice them?

YOUR HAPPINESS PLAN

_____

_____

_____

_____

_____

Narrow Focus: You need to focus on what deserves your time and attention. You need to focus on what you enjoy. And, above all, you need to focus on what will get you to your goals in the shortest time possible. In this digital age, with so many electronic distractions, it is very easy to get sidetracked and spread yourself too thin. Narrow focus is about avoiding those pitfalls and getting things done powerfully.

It starts with identifying what deserves your time and attention. What activities is your long term career growth most closely associated with. What would get you to your goals in the shortest time? What is it that the world needs most from you?

For example: when I am going to train a group of consultants on effective consulting skills, what they need the most from me is the training program. However, I do not need to spend 3 days designing the most beautiful slide deck. I can outsource it to a PowerPoint expert or delegate it to one of my team members. This is what doing what the world most needs from you means. I understand, this is not realistically possible for everyone but I am sure you can eliminate, transfer or outsource some low value activities from your life. These activities may include unnecessary meetings, unimportant requests, spending too much time on email, daily chores, etc.

The best metaphor which I think explains this idea is the one of the million-dollar race horse. If you had a million dollar race horse, how would you use it? Would you use it to bring grocery, moving furniture, etc. or would you take care of it and save it for what matters most – the race. I know you would protect it so it performs at its very best in the race.

The same principle should apply to you too – isn't it? You are your own million dollar race horse and your consulting practice is the race. You need to guard your energy, creativity and time for where it matters most in your work – everything else should either be eliminated or delegated. I call this the race horse mindset.

Another powerful strategy is what I call the legendary ninety. This refers to attacking your most important task of the day as the first thing in the morning while guarding your focus like a treasure. This is the time your mind is fresh and ready to provide you with the necessary mental energy required to accomplish any task. However, it is critical that you guard your focus and do not distract yourself with email or your cell phone at this time.

This will enable you to activate your creative genius in producing great work.

Tenacious Peddling: I've certainly observed it in my life, and I bet you've noticed the same: when things do not go in our favor, we have a tendency to slow down. Our productivity decreases. Sometimes we even give up. Clearly, this is not a promising route to optimum productivity. I learned how to deal with these situations using some wisdom shared with me by my grandfather. He is an extraordinary person and an inspirational figure in my life. He moved from Pakistan to India during the partition of 1947, in response to Pakistan being founded as an official Muslim nation. As a result, he was forced to start over from scratch in a new country. He bought vegetables from farmers and sold them door to door. In the evening, he studied under the streetlights.

He rose to all these challenges head-on and wound up as a university professor. He was also a keen cyclist. He often spoke to me in cyclist terms. One time he quoted Einstein to me, saying, just as a cyclist has to keep moving forward to maintain balance, in the same way, you need to continually move forward in life to maintain your balance. Only by persistently peddling can you move forward into that dream future that you imagine for yourself.

Remembering these wise words of this remarkable man, recalling all of that through which he persevered in those early years, when things are not working out well for me, I remind myself to just keep peddling. Keep moving forward toward my goal. Hence, I suggest to you, when you find yourself at one of those occasions where everything seems to be pushing back against you, when the results are not coming out as you had wanted, when the going gets tough, consider my grandfather's advice: keep peddling forward. If you can just keep going forward, tenaciously, eventually, you will arrive at that proverbial light at the end of the tunnel.

This completes our discussion of the second component in this chapter on personal mastery: understanding productivity. The clues I've provided for understanding and mastering productivity, here, neatly organize into the acronym COUNT: reminding us of my mother's great advice that we make every day count. These clues were:

- **Cheerful Associations**
- **Olympian Planning**
- **Undefeatable Happiness**
- **Narrow Focus**
- **Tenacious Peddling**

If you can manage to follow these valuable clues, then you will be successful at making each day count and will make great strides towards the constant improvement of your productivity. This brings us to the third and final component of personal mastery.

Managing Stress

Stress is a part of our day to day life. As a consultant, you will often find yourself constantly facing more challenges as compared to any other professional. This, in turn, can lead to stress. So it becomes imperative for us to understand and manage stress effectively. In fact, our ability to manage stress over a longer-term has a direct impact on our achievement and our success in the consulting profession. Let's begin with understanding what stress is and where it comes from. Once we have done that, then we will get into some proven best practices to manage stress in our lives.

Now, what is stress? In the simplest terms, stress is our reaction to an undesired outcome or our reaction to the fear of an undesired outcome. Sometimes, stress does not necessarily need anything to happen – just the fear of something happening can lead to stress. We run into difficulties every single day. These can be challenges at work, the fear of not meeting a deadline, the fear of not meeting client expectations, making critical decisions, changing requirements, dealing with complex projects, etc. Stress can even come from building your business, if the business is not growing at the pace you want. Stress can also come from your personal life. Clearly, there is stress from all areas of life. Now, how do you effectively manage stress so it does not impact your life? We are going to look at five best practices to effectively manage stress as a consultant.

1. The first one is *exercise*. As we discussed, exercise is something that has multiple different benefits. It impacts not only your health but also your mental health. It impacts your performance, it impacts your productivity - it impacts all different areas of your life. When you exercise, you release good chemicals like endorphins, which increase your endurance to stress, along with making you feel good about yourself.

2. The second effective strategy for dealing with stress is *deep breathing, coupled with mindfulness*. Mindfulness and deep

breathing are gaining a lot of traction in the business world off lately. Some of the most influential leaders in business and in the business world are adopting this practice on a regular basis. So what is this? Deep breathing coupled with mindfulness is simply consciously relaxing and focusing on your breathing. You can do this exercise right now. Sit where you are, in a comfortable position. With your shoulders relaxed, your hands on your lap and your feet resting comfortably on the floor, focus entirely on your breathing. Close your eyes and actually observe the breath of air go into your nose. Focus on the air leaving your lungs through your mouth or nose. Keep focusing on exhaling and inhaling. It is normal to get distracted when you do this. Remember to bring your attention back to your breathing whenever you catch your mind wandering off. Adopting this practice even for three minutes a day has shown to reduce stress. This is a game changer. If you want somebody to guide you through it, you can easily find some clips on YouTube; just search for "mindfulness exercise."

3. The third strategy is *nature walks*. I cannot emphasize the benefits enough of going out in nature often. Get your blood flowing, get pure oxygen in and catch some beautiful views along the way. Try to get some sun and break a sweat. Remember to metaphorically stop and smell the flowers. Spending time with nature is something that will reduce your stress levels almost immediately.

4. The fourth strategy is *music*. Music completely transforms your attitude, your perception of life at that given moment. You have probably listened to a piece of music that

got you pumped up. You might have listened to another piece of music that made you lazy, you wanted to go to sleep or actually slept. Music has a significant impact on your body, your mindset and on your overall energy. The right kind of music to deal with stress would be something that pumps you up, makes you feel inspired, increases your energy, etc. Try this out the next time you feel stressed. It is very effective.

5. The final strategy is my favorite and is something that can have a long-term impact on your stress levels and almost shield you against it. This is what I call *focus-shift*. This is when you transform your focus from being a victim to that of a warrior. As we discussed, stress comes from your response to an undesired outcome or the fear of an undesired outcome. This could mean that you are putting yourself in the victim zone; you are thinking that bad things are happening to you; you are not getting the right results; the right things are just not happening – you end up in the victim zone where you feel things are happening to you and not for you. This could make you feel stressed, depressed, stuck, lethargic and low in energy. On the other hand, the warrior focus is where you say and think that "I am in control of things," "Even if things did not turn out the way I would like them to, I could transform them," "I can change them," "I can improve my effectiveness in this," "I can learn from this." This is the warrior mindset.

Warrior mindset is a mastery mindset. Warriors learn things and become masters rather than being dabblers. A warrior is someone who is focused on growth rather than results, somebody who is willing to take risks rather than being stuck in that familiar, safe place. As our focus shifts from being a victim, where things are happening to you, to being a warrior, where things are happening for you, stress levels dip. If you can embrace this focus-shift, if you can consistently stay in the warrior zone, if you can constantly focus on learning and mastery, if you can consistently focus on your pursuit of being a legendary consultant, stress would disappear. You would see positive things happening, you would see that you are in control, you would see that you are producing every single result that you aimed for. You are in control of your life because your life is a reflection of who you are. This is the final stress management strategy. Most, if not all of the top consultants practice this.

To review, stress is something that we can very effectively manage. There are a lot of proven practices that help us manage stress including exercise, deep breathing with mindfulness, taking nature walks, listening to music and finally, shifting our focus from being a victim to being a warrior.

Make a note of the practices you would add to your regular weekly schedule to keep your stress levels in check.

Your Stress Management Plan

_____
_____
_____
_____
_____
_____
_____

Rocket Fueling Your Growth with a Mentor

As human beings, it is in our nature to see the world through the lens of our own perception. It does not come naturally to us to see the world through the eyes of others, to walk in their shoes. This fact about humans though turns out to offer a leveraging opportunity, which enables you to rocket fuel your growth. This opportunity is having a mentor. It is because such a mentor can see you, your situation and actions, through a lens both distanced and less partial than the lens through which you are capable of seeing yourself. Your mentor's feedback helps you gain a new perspective on the industry and navigate your personal performance within it. Mentors provide fresh insights and evaluations and thereby help you make better decisions. A mentor is someone who has already been there and done that. They give you a leg up: the edge that rocket fuels your growth into the top one percent of consultants.

Benefits of Having a Mentor

All great consultants have had mentors at some point in their lives. I have had the honor of being mentored by some of the smartest people in the industry. These are among the most intelligent people I know in any walk of life. They have had a significant impact on my life and my consulting career. They've even contributed to the quality of this book. I can't overstate the value of these kinds of relationships in your life and consulting business and strongly urge you to seek out such relationships. They are profound difference makers.

Let's consider some of the key benefits of having a mentor more closely:

1. First is the benefit of *knowledge,* the opportunity to tap into previously unmined knowledge reserves. If you've chosen wisely, these are people who have had experiences and learned truths about the industry which you've not yet achieved. This is knowledge which you don't have access to or awareness of but can make a huge difference by saving you from costly trial and error mistakes. Likewise, they can provide you with insight into unanticipated problems within your industry or specialization. All this helps you improve performance and efficiency.

2. Another, often underappreciated, benefit of a mentor is the *reduction of loneliness and isolation*. Being a legendary consultant can be an isolating experience. You're starting your day earlier than most people, you're often working harder and longer hours to add more client value than most people, and much of your so-called spare time is spent on value-added business activities, which often are done in isolation. That kind of isolation can breed feelings of loneliness. As Aristotle famously observed, we humans are social animals. And if you don't believe ancient philosophers, evolutionary psychology has come to the same conclusion (Alexander, 1974, 1982). Loneliness is a signal that we've been isolated too long. A strong mentor relationship can really make the difference in overcoming that loneliness. We feel like we are a part of an ongoing team, with a common purpose, to improve performance and productivity. This feeling of belonging and sharing makes a huge difference in our emotional and psychological health.

3. Another underappreciated benefit of a mentor is *accountability*. Setting goals is extremely important. But if we fail to reach those goals, we tend to fudge them in our mind, make excuses, even misremember what we said, or ignore the possible consequences. A mentor though, who is committed to aiding us in our success, can be the necessary voice of accountability: the person who reminds us when we have let ourselves down. Even more importantly, they are the concerned, but honest people you'll have to face if you fall short of your goals. Well-meaning and fair-minded accountability can be a powerful motivator

4. Also, extremely important in the mentor relationship is *honest, constructive feedback*. None of us like to be criticized, but when the criticism is coming from someone who you know has your best interest at heart, it is possible and immensely beneficial to hear the undistorted truth. What do you not do well? How can you improve? Why is a particular strategy failing? We often have a hard time being honest with ourselves about answering these kinds of questions, and we don't readily accept the criticisms of those we do not trust. A trusted mentor is invaluable in providing you the feedback to continually improve yourself toward your goal of legendary consulting.

All of these benefits are of immense importance, and none of them are things that you can achieve on your own. By definition, they require the input of someone outside of your perspective and experience. This is why I say that finding that trusted, experienced and committed mentor is the key to rocket fuelling your growth as a legendary consultant.

How to Find a Mentor?

Now, before you start looking for a mentor, you need to *identify what kind of a mentor you need*. Do you need someone with lots of experience in your field, who can help you make the tough decisions in navigating your career or do you need someone who is a master of the trade, who, regardless of their own area of specialization, have mastered the skills necessary for legendary success and can aid you in your efforts to master your skills?

This is not necessarily the same person and certainly not with the same focus. Other types of mentors are those with a strong associational influence: these are mentors that can help you expand your all-important network. Some people simply need a mentor who can provide effective moral support: someone who listens and encourages them through the tough times.

Different potential mentors have different strengths. Some are great at soliciting new clients and driving the business forward but aren't as strong at executing the work. Likewise, of course, there are the opposite: those with robust analytical skills, but whose social skills aren't sufficient to build strong business relationships. Identifying the right mentor for your needs is important. Who will bring to the mentor relationship the insights and skills from which you would most benefit?

Once you've identified your own needs in a mentor, the challenge is to *find the right person*. It would be a mistake though, to allow this necessary evaluation process to mislead you into an epic search, turning every stone in every corner, to find just the right fit for your mentoring needs. In truth, it's highly likely that the right mentor for you is already someone easily identified from within your professional circle. Look into your circle and make a note of those who are strong in the skills that you want to improve. They don't have to be world champions; as long as they are better than you, as long as they have valuable lessons to teach you, they can be a great mentor. Nor, is it a matter of their formal qualifications, their position or title. Sometimes your peers, those at the same point in their career as you, can have something valuable to offer you.

Now comes the tricky part: *how do you get such a person to mentor you?* The secret formula is this: you simply ask. You chose them as a desirable mentor for a reason. Simply tell them so and why. Say you respect and admire their work in this particular area and you'd really like to improve your own efforts. Of all the people in the field that you know, tell them they are the ones from whom you feel you could learn the most. Ask them if they would sit down with you occasionally and provide some feedback. Maybe ask them to tell you about their learning curve: what experiences, led them to essential lessons, which really made the difference in refining their skills. This is what I recommend as the standard approach, and it can be replicated and scaled for both the number of skills you want to improve and your own increasing proficiency in those skills. This should be regarded as the default method for identifying and seeking personal mentors.

Occasionally though, in particular circumstances, there may be sound reasons for *hiring a paid mentor*. This is someone you pay a fee for their help in improving an area of your consulting business. You usually hire such a person when you have a narrowly identified skill that you need to grow quickly and sharply. In that case, it may make sense to find someone who is a true master of that skill and pay them for specific deliverables. These typically are people who coach consultants as a part of their own business. These coaches can usually bring up the level of your game more dramatically and immediately compared to what can be accomplished by working informally with someone who is one or two rungs up the ladder from your own abilities. These paid mentors might be something to consider, for instance, if a unique consulting opportunity has presented itself and you know that the only way of taking advantage of that opportunity is to very quickly establish a sharp increase in your current skill level in a specific area of practice. Presentations, public speaking, selling, and a variety of other areas are skills that commonly experience dramatic and immediate improvement with the right professional coaching. These paid mentors dig deeply into your own individual case and use their expertise to tailor the right solutions for you.

To review: how do you find a mentor? First, identify the kind of mentor you need. What are your specific needs: improved skills? If so, which ones? Or, maybe you need social connection and moral support. Once you've identified your need, look around you, in your social circle, for someone, a colleague, a peer or a classmate, who possesses ability in the area you admire and would like to benefit from or emulate. Then it comes down to asking them in a way in which they feel appreciated. Finally, in particular, unique circumstances, it can make sense to hire an expert in a specific skill you need to quickly and sharply improve.

Please think of professionals in your industry that you think could prove to be great mentors for you, and decide on a date and time to reach out to them.

Your Mentorship Plan

_____

_____

_____

_____

_____

A final consideration I'd ask you to reflect upon in this discussion of mentorship is that mentoring takes two. It's a two-way street. There will be those around you whose skills you admire and from whom you'd like to learn, just as inevitably there will those who admire and want to learn from you in some skill area. I would encourage you to be open to being a mentor yourself. You can be confident that those who agree to mentor you have benefited from the mentorship of others: maybe in that same ability or maybe in another area. But mentorship is a circle of mutual benefit. As others help you become a better consultant, you are also called upon to help others.

Again, don't think that you need to be a master in some skill or super successful in your practice. As long as the person asking for your mentorship believes they have something valuable to learn from you, you are presented with an opportunity to give back and repay the help others offered to you. We consultants, remember, are in the business of adding value to the lives and businesses of others. Mentoring is another great way to be able to accomplish this.

Sometimes all it takes is being open to providing someone feedback, some suggestions on how they can improve. In some situations, say if you're a mentor to someone on a team of which you are the leader, you can provide them the opportunity to rise to the occasion, to prove to themselves they can do what they may have doubted their capability on. Sometimes it's simply being willing to sit over a coffee once in a while and listen to their doubts and anxieties, being willing to share your own stories about how you overcame similar obstacles. We're all human, and as such, we can all inspire each other to be our best.

I believe that this is an under-considered aspect of legendary consulting. At our best, we are not only succeeding for ourselves, but we are also succeeding with and for others. Giving back as a mentor can be an important part of achieving that legendary status.

In this chapter, we've reviewed the nature and importance of personal mastery. This is the starting point of legendary consulting. Mastering your lifestyle, making good personal choices about how you live your life; mastering your productivity, with the appropriate ideas, mindsets and strategies; managing stress, with effective techniques; and developing a trusted, committed mentoring relationship, that encourages you to learn, be accountable and integrate feedback: these are the cornerstones of personal mastery. This is the hard work in becoming a legendary consultant. After you've mastered these challenges, everything else is much easier.

« CHAPTER THREE »
Proposal Mastery

"The salesperson you'd ideally like to be and the salesperson you'd like to encounter as a customer should roughly be the same, shouldn't they?"

- CHRIS MURRAY

The previous chapter on personal mastery covered the fundamentals that will lay the foundation for effective consulting work, allowing you to perform like a legendary consultant. That performance though does require some elite skills. The next several chapters aim to help you develop those skills that will allow you to consult like the top one percent.

The profession of consulting heavily relies on abilities to compile, craft and present compelling work proposals in aid of the client's interests. Consulting is a service provided to clients. Sometimes it is the client who comes to you, recognizing a need that they have. In the highly competitive modern world though, more often than not, the onus is on you to take your message to potential clients. In such cases, it is up to you to provide a compelling pitch and close the deal. Proposal and presentation skills are essential for achieving these ends.

Indeed, this also applies when the clients come to you. You still need to convince them that you are the one for the job, you can provide the service and solution they need, you can offer the value they're seeking, and it makes sense for them to hire you. Doing that consistently and successfully requires top-level proposal and presentation skills. Compiling and presenting captivating proposals is the first client-facing challenge of successful consulting, and there's no doubting or disputing the exceptional importance of these skills.

Yet, despite their evident importance, my observations from being in the industry all these years have been that even the best-intended, well-meaning, and most earnest consultants often lack both the skills necessary and an appreciation of what they're missing out on with this skills deficit. They struggle to produce and present a package of compelling proposals. It's in response to these ongoing challenges that this chapter offers to guide you in crafting and presenting consulting proposals like the top one percent do. It is also worth mentioning that a proposal referred to here is not something you submit in a request for proposals (RFP). Those are different and need to follow the structure and content details outlined by the receiver.

Many of the concepts discussed here will overlap with the related concepts of sales. This is not a coincidence or lack of conceptual distinction. In fact, when you are presenting proposals you are selling an idea. You may be confident that if your client understands your idea, they will want to buy it, but the responsibility is on you to present your approach to the client in such a way that they recognize the value it provides. That recognition alone will be the reason they choose to buy what you're selling. The decision maker has to find the idea in your proposal easy to understand. This should be obvious. Even more so, your selling job has to inform and inspire the decision maker, which leaves them ready for taking concrete action on the idea. Instilling such commitment and triggering such inspiration to action is your job.

So, no matter how great your idea is; how much value it offers to the client; if that client rejects the idea, there's no point lamenting over the client's short-sightedness or lack of sophistication. The problem isn't with the client, it's with your failure to convey that greatness and value. It was your job to sell to the client; if the client didn't buy, it was you who failed to make an adequately compelling sales pitch. You didn't communicate the idea well enough for them to act on it. It's never the client's job to say yes. It's your job to inform, empower and educate the client to an understanding that has them wanting to say yes.

The Three Types of Proposals

Let's begin then with an overview of the types of proposals that consultants create. The first of these that I want to consider is *the new project proposal*. This could refer to the proposal of a project with a new client or to the proposal of a new project with a current or past client. There are of course, significant differences in these. When you're proposing to a current or past client, you're dealing with someone with whom you have a track record. This is someone who knows that you can add value to their company and you'll deliver what you promise. Proposing a project to a new client still requires a bit of selling to someone who has not got a track record working with you.

The second type of project proposal is the *new side project*. In this case, you're actively working with a client in an ongoing project, and you recognize an opportunity. This would be something that grows organically out of the ongoing project. It can be the opportunity to leverage an initially unplanned opening, or it could be a response to an unanticipated challenge arising from the ongoing project. In some way, the new side project is a logical extension of the current project. When well thought through, these kinds of side projects can be a great win-win. They certainly generate more work for you without having to go out in search of new clients, but they also allow the client to build on current improvements, leveraging their sunk cost for an even higher return on investment. When well-conceived, the new side project can be a major benefit all around. The success rate of such proposals is typically much higher than other proposals.

An example of this would be a company that hires me to consult on building a business plan for a new product X that can be used to win over new investors and secure funding. They might turn out to be interested in a side project on how to improve their development plans for product X. Or, I might be able to help them with a framework for selecting and connecting with top-level raw material suppliers for product X. This kind of a side project not only adds direct value in strengthening the original business plan, for which I was hired initially but also aids in the client's broader business strategy and their ongoing operations.

The third type of proposal is the *follow-on proposal*. Just as it sounds, these are proposals for helping your client make the next step following the successful completion of a prior project. This could entail implementation or fine-tuning of the work done earlier or the opening up of a new opportunity horizon, made possible by that earlier work.

The ideas we'll be examining as we move forward will apply to all three of these different types of proposals. I've reviewed them so that you can picture in your mind the different contexts

3 - Proposal Mastery

within which these ideas can be applied. It's important to maintain this context as you consider the approach to proposal mastery. Sometimes we do not make enough work proposals. This shortcoming simultaneously leaves us with insufficient work and denies our clients the complete possible value they can obtain from our skills and experience. So, as we're thinking about how to master proposals, keep in mind that using that mastery to optimize business opportunities and benefit your clients' value-added propositions is the full achievement of our proposal mastery.

After all, a huge part of being a legendary consultant is about bringing in lots of business. And there's a great benefit to you in this with regards to making your life as a consultant more rewarding. The more effective you are in making proposals, the more business you bring in, the more interest you can generate among potential clients, the more selective you can be in which jobs you actually do take. You can choose the ones that inspire you, where you'll be able to learn and grow, aligning yourself with the achievement of the personal mastery goals discussed in the earlier chapter. And, it goes full circle: the more selective you can be, the better you'll be able to focus on the work that inspires you and at which you excel, then, in that way, you'll be most proficient at bringing the highest level of value to your clients. This is the path to being a legendary consultant.

It all starts with effective proposal writing. This is a central pillar of the legendary consulting system.

Right Attitude for Proposal Writing

Let's now consider the right attitude for composing a compelling proposal.

1. The first aspect of that attitude, which is essential, is *a client-interest focus*. You must always remember to keep the client's interest at the center of your proposal. The key to success in this is for you to really understand what the client wants. What matters to the client? What are their fears and hopes? Their aspirations and dreams? When you know that you can create a proposal that speaks right to the heart of the client's interests, you can create a proposal that matters to the client.

   Remember, as frequently discussed in the pages above, the key to legendary consulting is adding tangible value to your client's life and business. This aspiration has to inform and animate your proposal. Consultants can sometimes get sidetracked, tempted to propose projects that may not be what the client needs: may not add value to their life or business. Some consultants might do that out of financial interest or even mere vanity. Whatever the reason, it is a trap that in the long run helps no one; we all have to be on guard against that trap. Making a conscious effort to keep the client's interest as the central focus of all your proposals is the best way to avoid falling into that trap. It is a critical attitude that you will slowly cultivate. It strengthens over time.

2. The second aspect of developing the right attitude for legendary consulting is having *no fear of selling the right thing*.

3 - Proposal Mastery

Proposal writing is selling an idea. You have an idea that you believe in as a benefit to the client's life and business. You want to sell that idea to the client. You want to show them how it will benefit them. As a legendary consultant who believes in your ideas, in what you're proposing, and its value to your client, you should not be scared to sell. Remember, selling is essentially the transfer of belief. If you truly believe that your idea, your service, strategy, plan, product, etc. will help the client improve their life or business, it is your responsibility to sell it. And to not be afraid to sell it. Wouldn't you want someone to do the same for you?

Now, when I say "sell," I do not mean forcing or manipulating them to buy your idea. I do not mean hard selling. I don't mean chasing the client down the street (figuratively or literally). I mean passionately proposing your ideas, giving them the full range of your conviction. If you believe in what you're proposing and are not afraid to stand behind it, that passion and conviction will shine through. Your client will see it and be moved by it. If you honestly and truly believe the idea that you're proposing will make your client's business better, it is your duty to try to move them to action. You can inspire and empower clients to act if they see and feel your belief that your proposal will make their business better and that you've been attentive to the importance of keeping their interest front and center. That's what selling in a consulting context is: *inspiring others through your conviction and passion for the solution you propose, to help them eliminate their business and life challenges.*

Naturally, there can be other constraints, such as the availability of resources and time. Experience has taught me though, that when the idea is strong when the consultant believes in the idea, when it's communicated with passion and clarity, clients find a way of making it happen. So, do not be afraid of selling the right thing.

3. Third, *put in the work*. A lot of work goes into creating a compelling proposal. An essential part of having the right attitude for legendary proposals is being willing to put in all that work. You have to research the market, the client's business – past performance, financial statements, etc.; industry standards and trends. There's a lot of work that goes into gathering the information you need. All this work can be daunting. As consultants, we need to put in all this work without there being any guarantee that our prospective client will actually green-light the project we're proposing

As a result of these realities, there is the temptation to minimize your potential losses from a prospective client's thumbs-down by putting in as little work as you can get away with doing. This is a perfectly understandable risk avoidance strategy. But this is not the attitude of the legendary consultant. When you put in the work, it shows. It translates into belief. It translates into awareness of the client's business. It translates into the passion that moves a project forward. When the client can see that you understand their business and industry, they will be much more comfortable moving forward with your proposal.

Furthermore, putting in the work vastly increases the likelihood that your efforts won't be an investment without return.

That the client will see the proposal's merits and give it the green-light. Putting in the work is the best way of avoiding the very risk of failure and lost investment that might mistakenly lead some to not put in the work. And, there's something else to consider. What if you do put in all that work, all those hours and effort, and the client still says no? Is it really a complete loss? A write off? Probably not. Most clients, even if they're unconvinced the idea is right for them, if you've put in the work, they'll see it. They'll recognize your level of commitment and passion. That will make an impression. And that's an investment that can pay off down the road. Maybe a need will arise later; who are they going to think about calling? You, who made an impression with your passion and hard work. Maybe a colleague will ask them to refer someone who might be able to help them with a business challenge they're facing. Again, the impression you make, by the work you put in, doesn't cease paying dividends just because that client, for that project, chooses to pass. It's important to see the big picture if you're to have the winning attitude of a legendary consultant. Reputation matters.

4. The fourth aspect of the right attitude for mastering the proposals of legendary consulting is to *make it easy for the client*. Effective and compelling proposal writing boils down to making it easy for the client to make the decision to move forward, making it easy for the client to say yes. Clarity results in positive decision making. This resonates with the science of proposal writing (Sant, 2003). Everything you do, everything you create, in your proposal, your guiding principle is to make it easy for the clients, given their level

of expertise and skills. You need to provide them with just the exact level of information they need to feel comfortable in moving forward with. It's not about making it fancy or sophisticated. Definitely, if you know the client has a specific skill set or level of experience that allows you to get into more depth and sophistication, of course, address those strengths. But all the bells and whistles and fanfare aren't going to help you, aren't going to make you look smart if at the end they leave the client cold, unclear and ultimately unpersuaded.

5. Also, *continuous improvement*, one of the messages that are at the core of this book, applies specifically to proposal writing. We all aspire to be legendary consultants, to be a part of the top one percent, but nobody, none of those top one percent, achieved their legendary status overnight. It is a continuous process of evolution: a determination to improve. And this is no less true in developing your proposal crafting and proposal presenting skills. A part of the attitude necessary for success is a commitment to continuous improvement: being able to reflect on the work you've done, honestly assessing its strengths and weaknesses and being open to how you can take it to the next level. So, even where your proposals do not result in a "yes" from the client, they remain extremely valuable as baselines, beginning points, from which you can build and improve. This is also where the relations of collegial peers and your mentors can be fundamental. Perhaps they can see things and provide you feedback to which you remain blind. Also, ask the prospective clients for feedback. Seek the help and sup-

port of everyone you can. Learn from it and integrate what you've learned into each new proposal. That's the heart of continuous improvement: just do it better every time.

So, the right attitude for compelling proposal writing involves maintaining a client-interest focus, having no fear to sell the right thing, putting in the work, making it easy for the client and continuous improvement. When you can integrate all these approaches on a consistent basis, you will have cultivated an attitude toward proposal creation which will put you on the path to legendary consulting.

What Makes the Difference

Let's distinguish what separates average proposals from those by the top one percent. From my experience and years spent studying the best, the following factors massively increase your chances for successful proposal writing. It isn't that it's impossible to have a successful proposal without taking account of all these factors. Achieving success without considering these factors though, is a low and unreliable likelihood. On the other hand, proposals that comply with these factors have massively high prospects for success. They are far more likely to get a "yes" from the client and bring you the business. What then, are these factors that are the keys to success?

1. The proposals of legendary consultants are *concise*. Being concise makes it easy for the client to understand and thereby makes it easy for the client to say yes. With regard

to the number of pages, I have noticed around 3 - 4 pages to be the sweet spot. There are a lot of distractions in the modern environment that hinder people's ability to focus on things. So, the tighter the proposal, the easier it is for the client to follow. Being able to follow makes it easier to understand and act on the information in the proposal. Your job as a consultant is to provide just enough information for the client to feel safe about making the decision to go ahead. Any extra information is mere fluff that can only cognitively overload the prospective client's thought process and distract the attention needed for getting to the core ideas in the proposal. So keep your proposals concise, crisp and to the point.

2. Another rule of thumb with regard to conciseness is that if required, you should be able to convey your proposal verbally in less than 45 seconds. This level of conciseness and brevity requires a great deal of clarity in your own mind about what it is that you're proposing. Big pages of text feel intimidating to many people. Sharp, clean, economic bullet points are far more effective. Make it easy to read, make it easy to focus on, make it easy to understand. This makes it easy to act on. Being concise and clear is critical to successful and legendary proposal writing.

The second factor that makes the difference in legendary proposal writing is maintaining *a logical flow*. I want to share with you a specific proposal structure. I'm not saying that this and this alone is the structure that will bring you success. Others can succeed, too. A vitally important quality of that structure though, and one that your proposal must possess, whatever structure you use, is the emphasis on having a logical flow. This makes it easy to follow, making it easy to understand, making it easy for the client to take action. So, let's break down this structure that does this for you and your client:

i. Begin with an *executive summary*. This summary should convey your key idea in 35 to 45 seconds or about 100 - 125 words. While it is presented first, the executive summary should be the final part of the proposal that you produce. It should come last because it must capture the totality of your idea and that idea must be complete before it can be fully captured. Trying to do the executive summary before the proposal is complete is premature.

ii. Next, you want to *address the business need*. The business need is either a problem to be solved or an opportunity to be leveraged. The business is either facing a problem: such as low profits, low customer satisfaction, increased input costs, etc. or an opportunity: new product markets have opened up, regional expansion options are present, etc. It is this business need that must be identified right from the start.

iii. Then you address *options*. What resources or venues are available to the client to solve the problem or leverage the opportunity? Showcasing this not only educates the client on the path you will take in your work but also makes them feel comfortable with your strategy. For example, if the client's revenue is decreasing, what are some of their options? The client might be able to increase prices, introduce new products, penetrate new regional markets, change marketing strategy, hire new sales people, etc. There are many ways to increase revenue. In writing your consulting proposal, you want to list the options available that you will analyze for meeting the identified business need. You don't want to focus exclusively on one. You don't want the client to think that you're fixated on any one solution from the start: your pet hobby horse. The client needs to know that you're aware of and will consider the full range of potential options for addressing the business need.

iv. Next comes the *project flow*. In this step, you walk the client through the entire project flow. How the consulting engagement would be structured. What are the different phases of work going to look like? What will the timelines be? What will be the reporting structure? What will be the governance plan? These are all simple ideas to talk about but matter a lot to your clients.

v. The next component is *results and Return on Investment (ROI)*. This component is the most important part of the entire proposal. This is instrumental in creating urgency in the mind of the client and helping them justify the investment. In this component, you will be discussing the resulting cash flows, return on investment, net present value, etc. with respect to the results, your work will generate. You need to carefully analyze the relevant inputs and outputs of the project work along with meaningful assumptions to make sure that your numbers are well-founded and robust. You need to have sol-

3 - Proposal Mastery

id evidence for every assumption you are employing. If the analysis is in favor of your consulting proposal, it will become very difficult for the client to say no.

vi. This brings us to *the "ask."* What do you ask the client to do? This is also very important and something that a surprising number of good consultants miss. You have to know what you want the client to do after listening to your proposal. It would be a mistake to think that it is self-evident once the analysis and ROI numbers have been presented. Certainly, our proposal tells the client what needs to be done; it does not though, invoke the action required to do it. As psychologists observe, we humans procrastinate (Burka & Yuen, 2008). Most of us prefer to delay making tough decisions. Perhaps we fear making the wrong choices; perhaps we hope the problem will solve itself. But, all else being equal, we'd rather push the decision off to a later date. This is why the "ask" is so important. It is about packaging everything you've discussed and asking the client to commit to taking action – to making the decision.

An "ask" might sound something like this: revenues have been decreasing; multiple options for increasing them have been identified and will be analyzed, including introducing new products, opening new markets, improving brand perception, and increasing the prices of the current line, etc. We also discussed the project flow which showcased that the entire project can be completed in the next 90 days. Based on our result and ROI analyses, we are confident that the right approach will revert your positioning as an industry leader and bring the project ROI to 274 percent; while failing to act on this opportunity might result in continued revenue decline, market share loss and brand dilution. Moving forward, we invite you to start working toward this challenge, so that we can collaborate in bringing your business' position back up to its optimum capacity through a recovery of its revenues. How do you suggest we move forward today?

In a tidy, concise summary of what had been identified as the need, I laid out a logical assessment of what might be the best means to get the business to where the client wants it to be, I include the project flow details and the results and ROI analyses, culminating in asking them to take action. It is simple, compelling and to the point. So, this structure, as I explained earlier, has a logical flow built into it. You identify the business need, whether that be a problem or opportunity. You briefly mention the full range of options available to address that need. Then you illustrate project flow, provide insight into the timelines and reporting structures, and conclude by explicitly asking the client to take the necessary action to address that business need. Each step logically follows from the previous one.

3. Third in our list of factors that increase proposal success is *business understanding and support material.* Before you can create an effective proposal along the lines just discussed, you actually have to understand the business and the industry your client is in and the factors that impact it. You need

to talk to them in their language, using references they'll immediately grasp. This requires understanding their business. And doing this requires that attitude discussed earlier of being willing to put in the work. You need to take the time to understand how they think before you present them with a proposal. This can be done by reading their company reports, reviewing their website, reading blogs, watching interviews of top leaders, etc.

Here are some questions you might want to start with to gain this business understanding:

i. What do they most care about?

ii. What does success look like to them?

iii. What are their business priorities?

iv. What do they fear?

v. What are they most concerned about?

vi. If there was one thing in the business they could improve, what would it be?

You may not be able to get a fully fleshed out answer to every one of these questions. The closer you can get to the right answer though, the better equipped you are to understand the business. You would be surprised at what difference a small tweak that this knowledge allows can have on the impact of your proposal. This is business understanding.

What about support material? This refers to the data you'll need to do the analysis that will get you to the best option for solving the business need. Such materials could include professional standards, industry reports, or market research.

These are very important. You might be surprised how often the clients themselves have not read those reports or studied that research. Even if you wound up suggesting similar solutions, without the backing of the support materials, your proposal would be much less persuasive to the majority of clients. If you put in the work, and do the research, backing your proposal with the required support material, in the client's eye, it isn't just you proposing this solution, it's the professional organization, the industry association, leading economists who researched the relevant facts, who are actually proposing your solution. You benefit from the credibility of the sources you research. This approach can make a dramatic difference in the perception and outcome of your proposal.

4. The fourth factor that will make the difference in your proposal is basing it on the foundation of *greed or fear*. Humans take action as a response to either greed or fear. This basic way of stating the matter makes it sound a little crude, but essentially this is right. For example, take someone who does a master's in business administration. Sure, they want to improve themselves and gain new knowledge, but the bottom line underpinning the decision is almost surely an expectation that the downstream effect will be an increase in their lifetime salary gains. This is what I mean by greed. Not necessarily a mean-spirited attitude, as some associate to greed, but still a desire to improve one's position and have more of something. Fear is the other foundational motivation. One might, for instance, faced with changing technology in the workplace, take an occupational training course,

on their own dime and time, in response to the fear that failing to keep up with the industry's technological changes could cost them their job, along with all the financial and emotional difficulties that come with such a loss. This is the kind of thing that I mean by a fear response.

So, broadly speaking, we are motivated either by greed (to get more of something) or fear (to hang onto something we have and don't want to lose). Though, generally, fear is a more powerful motivator than greed. We are more likely to act to prevent losing our jobs than to do something that will increase our salary. Consider your own reaction to these prospects. If I offered you one training course, let's call it course A, that would increase your salary by 25 percent when the economy is doing well, or course B, which would assure you would keep your job though, without the salary increase, even when the economy turned bad, which course would you take: A or B? Most people are going to take course B. Not losing what they do have is more compelling than the prospect of getting something they do not have. This has been one of the profound insights of behavioral economics (Kahneman, 2013; Tversky & Kahneman, 1974). A bird in the hand is worth two in the bush. The benefit of a salary increase is not as great as the cost of losing the job. In fact, this fear can be greater than the benefits of a salary increase up to thirty or even forty percent.

What then, is the foundation of a successful proposal? Your success depends upon an effective appeal to greed or fear *or both*. You could talk about making more money or about not losing market share or brand approval. This can be thought of as the classic carrot and stick scenario. To move the mule along we can dangle a carrot in front of its face or we can smack its rump with a stick. Probably though, the surest way of moving the mule along is to do both. Likewise, with your proposal, you need to address either greed or fear, but I have found the most effective and successful proposals are those that do both.

How is this done? On the one hand, you can talk about how to increase revenues (greed) and get more of something, while ensuring that the high standing of the company brand image is not damaged (fear) and they don't lose what they have. Remember, people want more of what they have or even don't have – profits, revenues, brand value, market position - but especially hate to lose what they already have – losing market share, decreasing revenues, reducing profit margins. Your proposal is stronger if you recognize and address both of these prospects as a part of your proposal's foundation. The example provided in the "ask" section of the logical flow component a few pages ago, also showcases this in play. Please refer to it. It's an unbeatable combination.

5. The next key factor in proposal writing that can distinguish you from the pack is *sentence structure and word choice*. Remember, your key motivation is to make it easy for the client to say yes. So, if you use language like "we have an opportunity to increase profit margins," it's upbeat and positive, emphasizing collaborative endeavoring and an opportunity. Business leaders are looking for opportunities. That's how business works. No business exists unless it has recognized some opportunity at some point in the past.

You're bringing to their attention the next one.

Another case of word choice would be "I invite you to..." in the place of "I want you to..." or "you should..." act on this idea. There's a subtle form of respect in choosing this kind of language. The same thing with saying "I believe the market will..." as opposed to "the market will..." or even "I think the market will..." do this. Expressions like "I believe" or "In my opinion" are much more confident and assertive than "I think." These kinds of subtle tweaks in word choice can have a big difference in how your prospective clients perceive you and your proposals. So, as you're writing your proposals, always make a point of re-reading, dedicated explicitly to re-evaluating the word choices you've made. Are they as powerful as they could be? Do they express both respect and confidence?

6. *Belief* is another important factor in writing compelling proposals. When you believe in something, it shows. Belief is not something you can expect to automatically arise from the casting of an idea or opinion. It is something that needs to be built. You need to sell your idea to yourself before you can expect to sell it to your prospective client. This takes time and effort. Always ask yourself, if you were the client, if you had to make the expenditure of hiring yourself to help implement your idea, would you spend that money? If you can ask and answer that question honestly, you'll have a great measuring stick for the effectiveness of your proposal. And, when your current iteration of the proposal falls short, you know that you need to do more. It's always going to be by doing more that'll make your proposal better and, in the

process, convincingly build up your own belief in the idea. When you get there, you'll know, and for the client, it will show. That will give the client the confidence to act on your proposal.

7. The final factor in making the difference for your proposal is the *presentation*. Effective presentation dramatically increases the likelihood of your proposal's success. Now, this is not necessarily the kind of presentation one does by standing up in a room full of other people. Even a one-on-one, personal conversation is a kind of presentation. Many of the points we've discussed above come back into play here. Presentations have to be clear, concise, crisp, easy to understand, focused, and to the point; that is what makes them powerful. These qualities increase the likelihood of proposal success.

A great presentation follows the same logical flow of the proposal. It starts with a high-level summary, goes into the business need, discusses the available options, explains the project workflow, results and return on investment, and ends with the "ask."

There are certainly very specific presentation skills that are also required to make the very best proposal presentation. These will be explored in greater depth in the communication skills mastery chapter.

To summarize the points we've covered in this chapter: the factors that make the difference in a successful proposal are conciseness, logical flow, business understanding and support material, the foundation of greed and/or fear, sentence structure and word choice, belief in your proposal and effcctive presentation. If you can master all these, you are on your way to proposal mastery: producing the kind of legendary proposals that raise your game up into that of the top one percent.

« Chapter Four »
Relationship and Positioning Mastery

"If you believe business is built on relationships, make building them your business."

— Scott Stratten

Consulting is fundamentally a relationship business. And, above all, it's concerned with relationships of trust. It involves working closely with someone, trying to understand their business, their life, and their challenges, all with the intention of helping them improve. Your success in consulting is closely related to your effectiveness in relationship building and personal positioning. What your clients think of you and how you position yourself in their minds will make a significant impact on the overall outcome and success of your consulting work.

In the consulting business, all revolves around the client. Everything we do is aimed at creating value for the client. It should be evident that successful consulting requires the capacity to develop strong relationships with clients. These lead to the client trusting the consultant and valuing their contribution, to the extent that they are willing to recommend the consultant to others. Referrals are, after all, the lifeblood of a successful consulting practice. So, in the language of our industry, your goal as a consultant is to successfully position yourself as a trusted advisor to the client.

Consider for a moment the term trusted advisor. This phrase has lately risen to the level of industry buzz word. Don't allow your understandable and healthy skepticism about marketing jargon though, to obscure the fact that this objective, becoming a trusted advisor, is the time-honored heartbeat of legendary consulting. Your success in bringing value to the lives of others is entirely dependent upon them believing in you as an advisor who has their best interest in mind and at heart. This bond of trust is not to be regarded casually or taken for granted: trust is a feeling that needs to be earned in the forge of personal experience. People trust you when their experience tells them you're worthy of their trust.

Key Practices for Effective Relationship Building and Positioning

There are specific practices you can follow that will facilitate the process of a client learning to trust you. I'll discuss nine key practices for effective relationship building and positioning here:

1. The first such practice is *building rapport*. Rapport is the feeling of connectedness with someone. It is the foundation of effective communication and relationship building between two people. Rapport is often the difference between two people enjoying a conversation or not. Having the right rapport with someone sets the

tone for building and strengthening the relationship going forward. While rapport may be a somewhat ephemeral idea, it is a perfectly concrete aspect of relationships and can be nurtured through a specific set of strategies. So, let's begin by examining these strategies:

i. *Mirroring* is a technique recognized by psychology in the early 20th century and is something that is studied even today (Iacoboni, 2009). In a nutshell, the central finding of this discovery is that people like people who are like them. This is why it is common to see people with shared cultural and ancestral backgrounds gathering together for rituals, social and even commercial occasions. They share common behavioral and attitudinal shorthand, making them feel at ease around each other. Mirroring works on this human disposition. It allows you, standing or sitting in front of another person, to trigger this cognitive process that conveys the recognition that you are someone like them. Effectively, their individual categorizing mechanism is stimulated to include you in their in-group, which by definition is, a part of their circle of trust. If this sounds manipulative, be aware that most of the time, in fact, we're mirroring other people subconsciously, just as they are prone to doing the same toward us. Consider how natural and yet completely different the way you'd talk to a 5-year-old child and a 45-year-old CEO is. Vocabulary, cadence, tone of voice, body language, etc. all these things are instinctively adapted to the individual who we're addressing. That is mirroring. We constantly mirror. Here though, my emphasis is on some techniques that you can consciously employ, which, with enough practice, will eventually also become automated, natural mirroring behavior.

Communication style is the most important aspect of mirroring. How you speak and sit; your posture, gestures, pace, personal space: all these things are a part of your communication style. For example, if the person you're talking to speaks in a subdued tone of voice, but your tone is loud, fast and exuberant, you're likely to make them feel uncomfortable. Whether they can articulate the reason for their feeling or not, the impression they'll take away is that you're not like them. They might consider you brash and even arrogant. Likewise, if they have a more extroverted style, but you speak in a subdued tone, they may take you to be timid or even unconfident. In either case, they perceive, consciously or not, that you're not really like them. The same goes for hand gestures. Some people are inclined to grand gesturing while others are prone to sit on their hands, at least figuratively. In the same way, at least subconsciously, people interpret the behaviors of the other kind of communication style as suggesting something about that person which makes them different, subconsciously categorized as not being a part of their in-group. So, it is important to note the communication style of your prospective and actual clients and make a point of aligning your own style with theirs. This will help you establish the rapport essential for building a relationship of trust.

ii. The second important strategy for building rapport is *connecting on common ground*. This strategy too, taps into the foundation of mirroring effect: people like people who are like them. Being like them need not be based only on how you are, it can be about what you share. This is the role of creating common ground. What happens when you first meet someone? Likely you start off with an open conversation, which might be called small talk. This talk though isn't really so small in its value. While it might be of short duration, its contribution to building rapport can be immense and enduring. People will often ask others about their background, where they grew up, which school they attended, or in what part of the town they live. All these kinds of questions present opportunities for establishing common ground. Maybe it turns out that you're practically neighbors. Or perhaps you went to the same university as the client's brother-in-law. It turns out that these commonalities, even small ones, can be influential factors in triggering the sense of belonging to some shared ground, having certain qualities of being in each other's in-group. This provides the basis for the beginning of a connection, friendship and rapport.

iii. As exciting as the experience of building common ground can be, a third important strategic consideration is *not getting ahead of yourself* and appearing too keen on establishing rapport. Being too eager can look desperate, which sets off warning alarms for many people.

If you seem too inquisitive, too determined, you can come off as disingenuous and in fact, generate feelings of suspicion, which directly undermine our primary goal, here: the cultivation of a trusting relationship.

iv. *Compliments* are another valuable strategy for creating rapport. This is not about shallow and phony flattery. Most people see through that pretty easily, and this too sets off warning alarms about your intentions and honesty. But surely you can find things that you sincerely admire or enjoy about the other person. Even something as elementary as complimenting someone on their suit or even their high-quality pen. You can mention how much you like it and ask where they got it. And infuse your compliment with sincerity by explaining why you like it. The color, the style, the craftsmanship, whatever it is: compliment them on their choice and good taste. Maybe you really enjoy the graphics they used in their PowerPoint presentation or the precise language used in their email. There's a good chance that anything you notice enough to compliment is something that they have put some thought and effort into refining. Your compliment then makes them feel valued for their taste and effort. This on its own generates feelings of pride and status, which helps establish a rapport between you, but additionally, your gesture to recognize what was important to them triggers the feeling that you're both the same kind of person: they're more inclined to subconsciously categorize you as a part of their trusted in-group.

v. Strategy five is simply: *listen*. This is crucial. People want to be heard and valued. The best way you can contribute both qualities to your client relationship is to really listen. It's not enough to just hear. You have to proactively listen and appear to be listening. Listening shows respect and appreciation. When the client recognizes that you're genuinely listening, they feel valued by you, which leads them to thereby appreciate you as someone they can have confidence and trust in. This is another important way of establishing that rapport central to the client-focused, trusting relationship. And, incidentally, not to be overlooked, active and attentive listening is a powerful technique for driving the conversation, through tactical use of appropriate questions, in the most fruitful direction. We'll discuss this further in the chapter on communications mastery.

vi. The final strategy discussed here for building rapport is a practice that can and should infuse everything you do as a consultant, and is a theme running through this chapter and this entire book: *preparation*. As emphasized above, while much mirroring and rapport building will happen naturally, to get the utmost out of your capacity to build rapport with prospective and actual clients, you want to have these strategies operating at optimum capacity. None of this will come naturally to you, overnight. These are behaviors that have to be cultivated, which means you have to prepare for getting the most out of them. This requires you to do your homework in all aspects of your consulting practice.

Know your material, be forthright and confident, have your deliverables in tip-top shape. All the mirroring or common ground seeking will contribute nothing to a strong rapport if you're not actually selling your value and providing that value to your client. At the end of the day, who your client trusts is the person who not only sells them but the one who fulfills their promises. That requires you to be prepared in all facets of your work.

2. The second practice you want to master for effective relationship building, and personal positioning **is the first impression**. A powerful first impression is critical to legendary consulting: the fact is, most of the time when we first meet our clients, they are not actually yet our clients. They are a prospect. Sometimes this entails meeting you to get to know you, to see a proposal presentation, or just as a general discovery discussion. Most of the time, your first meeting with a client is exploratory. It is therefore essential that you make a powerful first impression at this initial meeting. This will be key in your ability to close the deal. So, how do you make a powerful first impression?

   i. The first critical consideration is *your appearance.* Are you dressed professionally? Or are you dressed semi-casually, or even super casually? Is your hair disheveled or nicely combed? If you're sporting a beard, is it well-kept? A good rule of thumb is that typically you want to look better than the client. This is how you're going to position yourself as that trusted advisor. It's not likely that the client will want to seek advice from someone who appears less impressive than them.

We all know that impressions have a significant impact on what others make of us. If we seem less professional, it's quite likely that other professionals will regard us as less organized, competent and even less intelligent (Goudreau, 2012). There have been numerous studies and experiments that have testified to this collective wisdom, over and over again. You don't need a three-piece pin-striped suit, but you need to look clean, sharp and well-dressed.

ii. The second consideration is what I call *the first impression formula*. This formula helps you put together your first impression in a structured manner, making it easy it for the listener to receive the message you want to convey, while also optimizing its impact. Whenever you're meeting prospective clients for the first time, at some point you'll want to communicate to them the information in this formula. And, ideally, you'll want to do so in the same sequence. So what is this first impression formula? It goes as follows:

   a. *Client-focused why?* Why are you in the consulting business? Why should the market care about you? What is the value you add to the client's business? Why do you want to help people in their industry? Perhaps you want to help businesses reduce their operational expenses; to improve their efficiency; expand into new markets. Whatever your "client-focused why" is, think it through in advance and be ready to lead off your discussions with a clear statement of why you want to be their consultant.

This portion of the first impression formula might go like this: "I help medium to large scale businesses reduce their IT maintenance costs and serve their customers better by improving the effectiveness of their IT systems."

A good template for creating your "client focussed why" is this:

I help _____ *target market* _____ achieve _____ *this (a result your client wants)* _____ , by _____ *doing this* _____

Spend a few minutes and create your "client-focused why":

_____

_____

_____

_____

b. *Evidence.* It's one thing to know why you are in the consulting business; it's quite another thing to be confident that you can deliver on that mission. You want to provide evidence to prove you can deliver on the promise of your "why" mission. You could explain that you've worked with some of the most successful companies in the world, and cite some

4 - Relationship and Positioning Mastery

concrete examples from your experience to illustrate the point: Microsoft, Honda, GE, BMW, etc. You could explain how you reduced their expenses, drawing on concrete numbers, demonstrating the contributions you made to their increased productivity. This is the kind of concrete evidence, which if you have it ready, right from the first meeting, can make your declared "why" a much more powerful promise of what you can do for this particular prospective client.

This portion of the first impression formula might go like this: "I have worked with clients all over British Columbia. The last project I completed was with Honda, where I helped them improve their customer satisfaction scores by 17% by improving the responsiveness of their after sales follow-up and service process."

A good template for creating your evidence statement is this:

In my last project, I was working with _____ *client name or industry* _____ achieve *this*, by _____ *doing this (be specific)* _____

Spend a few minutes and create your evidence statement:

_____

_____

_____

c. *The service offering.* This is your opportunity to tell the prospective client about the services that you offer. In my own case, the services I cite are Operations Design, Change Management, and Process Improvement. These are the consulting services that I want to put in the forefront of my prospective client's mind. This allows me to tie back into my "client-focused why," evoking for the client a clear image of what I can do to positively impact their business. And, of course, as I'm doing this, I've already established the evidence that I can deliver the goods on this promise.

So, as you put all of these together, you are conveying all the right points in an easily understandable structure, therefore setting the basis for a powerful first impression that will yield dividends for the rest of your consulting relationship.

iii. Over the course of delivering these components of your first impression message, you want to showcase *commitment.* You want to illustrate that you're not just in the business for money. You have a higher calling, a mission which you are driven to deliver on. Everyone is in the business for money; everyone's in every business for money. That's basically what we mean by business. You don't want your prospective client though, to see you simply as another one of everyone. You want that client to see your commitment, that sets you apart, that makes you different. This is what you need to communicate to the client in the making of that vital first impression so you can position yourself as a trusted advisor and make a great consulting relationship.

So, the three key dimensions of making a powerful first impression are: making sure your appearance is appropriately professional for the occasion; effectively exercising the first impression formula: informing the prospective client of your "client-focused why" you're in the business, providing evidence that you can deliver on the mission entailed in that "why" and a service offer that shows how the successful pursuit of your mission offers them an opportunity to improve their business; and showcasing commitment to your vision. All of these together will propel your clients to accept you as their trusted advisor and see the positive impact you can make on their life and business fortunes.

3. The third strategy for relationship positioning is *informal socializing*. In the consulting business, we're used to meeting people in their offices or boardrooms. These are the usual places of doing business, but those environments have particular constraints associated with them. It can make a huge difference if you can expand the sphere of your social interactions. Meeting at a coffee shop, a restaurant, or even just for a walk in the park, can completely transform the nature and context of your relationship with someone. My own ex-

perience has been that there is a dramatic and instant shift in the quality of my relationship with someone once I meet them outside of the usual business context.

So, I invite you to consider how it may be possible to arrange for a coffee or a meal with someone, with the benefit of such a boost to your relationship. However, as important as this approach can be for effective relationship positioning, it is important to be sensitive to the client's or prospective client's reaction to such a suggestion. Not everyone is the same, and some people don't feel comfortable taking the relationship outside of the traditional workplace. If you sense resistance, do not press the matter. It's certainly fine to propose such a plan once or twice, but if, after those proposals, there is no agreement or commitment, if the client seems to be putting it off, probably they're not interested, so let the matter go.

4. The fourth dimension to this plan for improving your relationship positioning is *providing clarity*. Vitally important to remember is that clarity triggers security. Security is one of the six core needs that we identified earlier. Human beings crave security. We want to feel secure about our lives, our work, and our relationships. And your clients need to feel secure about passing influence over some important aspects of their business, into your hands. It is your job to help build the necessary feeling of security for them to trust you with these aspects of their business. You can achieve this by providing them with clarity about what it is that you will do for them and their business, and exactly how you would do it.

4 - Relationship and Positioning Mastery

It is important that you convey your exact approach. Walk them through the phases of the project and your goals in each of these phases, along with status reports as you proceed. All of this clarifies for the client what is happening, what you are doing, and what benchmarks to use as progress indicators. This clarity cultivates the client's feelings of security. Once they feel confident in how you're approaching your work with them, once they're secure that those aspects of their business they've put in your hands are indeed in good hands, that security bred from clarity will culminate in trust. Building trust, remember, is the core of effective relationship positioning.

5. The fifth strategy for effective relationship positioning is *being available*. How is this accomplished? Let's consider a practical situation: how long does it take you to respond to an email? I'm not one of those people who have some hard and fixed timeline, say, within the hour or even within a couple of hours. I do agree though, that there is a proper time limit for responding. You certainly should respond to any client email within 24 hours. This is the most commonly accepted standard in the business world. It is important that you are available for your clients. They may have a sudden, urgent issue to deal with, that requires your immediate insight and expertise.

Responding to a client's needs may well require you to go outside of your comfort zone and work overtime on solving the problem. Long hours and late nights are not unusual under such conditions. However, your ability to deliver at those stressful times, when the client is really feeling the pressure, has a considerable impact on their impression of you, your dedication to your craft and your commitment to helping their business. The client's estimation of who you are and what you have to offer can be completely transformed by your rising to the occasion at such times of crisis. So, be available, answer your emails in a timely manner and be a partner who can be relied upon when your client needs it the most.

6. The sixth practice for getting the most out of your client relationships is to *meet deadlines*. Little things in business can make a big difference. Likewise, it is with relationships. Missing a deadline isn't necessarily the end of the world. Life happens, and unexpected events can undermine the most conscientious and well-meaning effort. There's probably no one in any walk of life who hasn't missed one or two deadlines along the way. It happens. However, as human as it may be, never underestimate the potential effect that a missed deadline can have on a client's perception of you. This may seem unfair, but our perception of fairness is irrelevant to the client's perception of competence and commitment.

The other side of this coin is that you can have a powerful impact for good on the client's perception of you when you prove your ability to consistently meet your deadlines. A few things you do may have a more profound effect on the client's perception of you as competent, conscientious and committed, which invites the client's growing trust in you. So, I urge you to plan sufficient time buffers into your schedule whenever developing deadlines, to allow yourself to consistently deliver on your promised deadline. This will give you the best chance to position your relationship with your client toward one of trust and partnership. When the client is confident that they are dealing with someone who knows their stuff and delivers, they feel secure in their relationship with you, which cultivates in them trust that you're a worthy partner in their business.

7. Seventh is the need to *follow up* and keep in touch. Consultants are always concerned about finding new clients to sustain and enrich their own business. Agreed, this is a necessary focus of our industry. However, an overwhelming number of such consultants fail to do the most obvious thing toward this end: follow up with their recent clients. Presuming you've followed the advice offered in this book and delivered for your past clients, it is going to be much easier to get a new contract with someone who knows your work and commitment than to persuade someone without prior experience of working with you.

Following up is the key to tapping into these opportunities. My general rule of thumb is to follow up with past clients every four months. Connect with them; ask them how their business is doing; check in on the work you had previously done with them, is it still working well? It could also be helpful to mention a business article or new piece of research relevant to their company or the work you initially did for the client. Something along the lines, "I read about this new research, and it made me think about how this was something you might be able to integrate into your marketing approach, so I wanted to tell you about it; maybe you'd like to read it." These sort of themes make for an effective follow-up.

Counterintuitive as it may first seem though, the one thing I'm always sure not to include in a follow-up is to ask them if there's anything new or further I can do for them on a consulting basis. The point of the follow-up is to demonstrate to the client that you've continued to be aware of and concerned about the well-being of their business even after the conclusion of your formal arrangement. This approach continues to position your relationship as one of mutual interest, partnership and trust in the future. If you include a request for consideration of future work in the follow-up, however diplomatically it's phrased, the benefit of the follow-up is undermined: an expression of concern for the client's business is turned into a sales pitch on behalf of your business.

You may have the best of intentions; you may want nothing more than to be of service to your client. However, even the subtlest shift from a follow-up to a sales pitch can completely transform the client's impression of your intention and thus of you, and thereby reposition your relationship with that client in an unintended, undesired and unfortunate direction. Leave the topic of potential future projects for the client. Believe me, if you have done your work well, they will bring it up on their own.

So, keep in mind, there are plenty of conversation areas that can be appropriate for a follow-up. Ask them about their family if your relationship had been one that included discussion of such personal matters. Certainly, ask them about their company and their business. Even ask

4 - Relationship and Positioning Mastery

them about their life or their health if that's appropriate, based on your past relationship. However, do not make the mistake of inadvertently or unintentionally, turning your follow-up into a sales pitch.

8. The eighth key practice in relationship positioning is to *being patient*. Trust is something that builds over time. It is fueled by the consistency of long-term effective behavior. It is understandable that when you get started with a new client, they will not trust you enough to disclose all their business details. It is important though that during this relationship and trust building phase, you do not let your foot off the gas. It is important to continue focusing on the right thing and continue going the extra mile in delivering outstanding results. This will slowly take your partnership to the next level, solidifying the client's trust in your abilities and your character.

9. And, the ninth and final practice for effective relationship positioning and building is to *be real*. Humans are pretty adept at sensing when others are being disingenuous, and we seem to have a natural aversion to those who strike us as insincere or fake. Likely this is an evolved protection against being taken advantage of by others. As a social animal, this is a vitally important adaptation for dealing successfully with others while not being used by the unscrupulous. Cheater detection machinery seems to come with the human mind (Cosmides, Tooby, Fiddick, & Bryant, 2005).

This amazing human adaptive legacy though, works both ways. It protects you from the disingenuous, and likewise, it protects others from you when you're not being sincere.

This is why it is essential to be real in your dealings with people as a consultant. The research from a wide range of social scientists has revealed that it is important to be open to others, to share your feelings and to be willing to be vulnerable to cultivate what they call "prosocial behavior" (Mikulincer & Shaver, 2010). You'll earn more trust in one moment of conceding you don't know how to do something, than you ever will from a long litany of assertions of your omniscience. Say you don't know and promise that you'll find the answer. Willingness to make an extra effort is worth far more than the hollow proclamations of the know-it-all. Modesty and vulnerability demonstrate transparency, which highly promotes trust. Clients value these qualities far more than pretension and allusions of superiority. Being real generates security in clients that they're not being taken in by someone who is more glitz than grit. And, as we've seen, security is an important key to trust.

The same emphasis on being real is important in all aspects of your relationship and interactions with a client, or even a colleague. If you're trying to get to know them, be sincerely interested in finding out who they are. Don't pretend to be interested in them or their family; it only counts, it only works, if you really do want to know more about them. And why wouldn't you? This is a person who, for at least some limited period of time, is going to be an important part of your life. You'd expect them to think of you as a real human being, then why wouldn't you treat them the same way? In the end, your sincerity, or lack of it, will always show. So be real in your relationships with others, and they'll repay you with trust.

These then, are nine key practices that help us position our relationships in such a way as to earn the role of a trusted advisor among our current and prospective clients. Building rapport, making a powerful first impression, informal socializing, providing clarity, being available, meeting deadlines, following up, being patient and being real are the important ingredients we've reviewed in this chapter for the recipe to relationship building and positioning that creates a partnership of trusted advisor with our clients.

« Chapter Five »
Communication Skills Mastery

"The single biggest problem in communication is the illusion that it has taken place."
- George Bernard Shaw

It was the summer of 1998, in Chandigarh, India; I was in grade six at the time. I can still remember how keen both my parents were on the prospect of me participating in a public speaking school competition. They not only wanted me to participate, but they also wanted me to do well. They worked hard with me on creating that speech. The topic for the speech that was assigned to me was harmful effects of pollution. My school rented a community auditorium and organized the competition. I did not do very well back in that competition, which disappointed my parents. I recall asking them, why they were so focused on my participating and excelling in that competition. My father explained to me that confidence and competence in effective communication were critical to personal success in today's world. That was back in 1998. But my father's sage advice has lost none of its value; effective communication is as critical now as ever in contributing to one's success.

Communication skills are the most highly valued skills in today's business world. And nowhere is this truer than in the consulting profession. It is through effective communication of ideas that consultants are able to add value to their clients. Recommendations, findings, visions all rely on communication to take effect in the client's world. Communication is the core of consulting. Think about the importance and value of eye-hand-coordination in sports, like baseball, tennis or even car racing. It is the underlying skill that makes effective batting, volleying or driving possible. For consulting, it is communication that serves as that undergirding skill, which supports and makes possible the effectiveness of everything else that you do.

Time and again I've noticed that the most successful consultants, those in the top one percent, are not distinguished by their experience or education. Rather, they are the ones able to effectively communicate. They communicate with confidence and clarity. This gives them the ability to influence. The consultant who is a strong communicator has a critical edge on the competition. Networking, leadership, teamwork, selling a vision, all these core practices of the consultant are dependent on the effectiveness of your communication skills. Studies show that perceived leadership is greatly influenced by communication ability (Awamleh & Gardner, 1999). For anyone with long years in the consulting field, that finding comes as no news. In fact, I am yet to see a successful consultant, who does not have strong communication skills.

Don't be worried though, by the fact that effective communication seems to come more easily to some than to others. If you're one of those who struggles with your communication skills, don't be discouraged. As I will emphasize throughout this chapter, communications is indeed a skill. And, like any skill, it can be improved with attention and focused practice. Mastering these communication skills will allow you to position yourself as a leader and expert in front of your clients, teams, and colleagues. It is this ability that distinguishes the legendary consultants from the rest.

This kind of deft communication skill assures clients they're in good hands. As we've discussed in the last chapter, the feeling of trust on the part of the client is an important ingredient in the consultant's ability to add real and tangible value to the client's life and business. Warren Buffett in one of his interviews recently acknowledged that the one skill that can almost instantly increase someone's value by 50 percent is improved public speaking. From my personal experience, there's no doubt about the truth in Buffett's statement. A considerable amount of the great work I have done, of the great projects I been a part of, and the great results I have achieved, has been a direct result of the tremendous amount of work I've put into continually improving my public speaking and communication skills.

To reiterate, the good news is that these skills are learnable; with the right instruction, conscious effort, and focused practice you can improve your communication skills. You can become a better, more effective communicator. You can become a better leader, team player, and colleague; this is what enables you to add value to your clients' lives and businesses. This is what distinguishes the legendary consultants.

Let's consider the precise areas in which we apply our communication skills in the consulting business. As mentioned above, this is the core medium we use to deliver our consulting services. If we include written communication, which of course we must, then pretty much everything a consultant does with and for a client involves some aspect of communication. As a consultant, you will lead meetings, write emails, deliver presentations, conduct phone calls, sell your ideas, manage conflict and build relationships. Relationship building, in particular, has been emphasized in this book as a key part of successful consulting. Like all these other routine practices of consulting, the entire edifice is, from the ground up, built upon your capacity to communicate effectively.

This chapter will provide you lots of information, keeping in mind the incredible importance I've placed upon the refining of communication skills. This will be the longest and most elaborate chapter in the book. As I've repeated multiple times now (because it is so essential to appreciate), effective communication is at the very core of successful consulting; it's vital you get this right. You need to give it the attention and focus it requires. We will aim to do this by looking at communication from a variety of angles and specialties. We begin with a discussion of one-on-one business conversations. That discussion is followed by an examination of presentation and public speaking skills; leading effective meetings; email and phone communication; and, finally, communicating technical information to non-technical people.

One-on-one Business Conversations

The one-on-one business conversation is essential for the successful consultant, as we've discussed in a variety of places earlier, most notably in the chapter on relationship positioning. Here we will be diving into some very specific strategies and styles that will improve your business conversation skills and indeed, help your communication skills more broadly. It's in the one-on-one business conversation where the relationships are built, and the deals are made. This is where the rubber hits the road: disagreements are sorted, and conflicts are resolved. Four components of one-on-one business conversations will be discussed: the bullet point speaking framework, body language, listening and giving feedback.

Bullet Point Speaking Framework

Please allow me to ask you a question; what is easier to understand: a full page of undifferentiated text or a page of text organized into discrete paragraphs. Most people choose the latter: the page organized into paragraphs. Following the same logic, is the paragraphed page easier to understand or a page of well-structured bullet points? Most people find the bullet points easier to read. The same concept applies to our verbal communication. We can speak in a full page of text or in bullet points. Speaking in bullet points makes it easier for people to listen to us, to absorb what we're saying and eventually act on what we're saying. This practice of speaking in bullet points takes the business conversation to a whole new level of comprehension and implementation.

Now, how do you speak in bullet points? This is a practice I developed as a part of the legendary consulting system, and I call it the Bullet Point Speaking Framework (BPSF). Obviously, technically, bullet points refer to a form of text formatting, but the main idea remains relevant for speaking in conversations. You want to organize what you have to say in easily digestible chunks and deliver them discretely. The point is to assist the listener to receive your message, understand it and ultimately act on it. Let's break down the BPSF into its functional units.

1. *Structure:* Any effective business conversation – with a client, teammate, colleague, etc. – is premised on building the right structure for the intended message. For example, if my client asks me: "Himanshu, how are we going to proceed with this project?" The first consideration in crafting my reply is how the response should be structured. The idea here is to recognize how the material that forms my reply is organized efficiently into easily communicated chunks. The precise number of chunks isn't important, but making them easily digestible is. Preferably though, I do want to keep the number of chunks down to an upper limit of five. Beyond five, it gets more difficult to follow and maintain. Answering that client, asking about moving forward, I could reply along these lines: "Moving forward, we have three main areas to work on:

    i.   First, research surveys;
    ii. Second, focus groups;
    iii. And, third, analysis of the gathered information."

In this way, I've chunked the response into three separate categories. Consider how my response might have sounded had I not structured it appropriately. I might have said: "Yeah, there are multiple things we should do; we've done good work in the past, but moving forward we would have to do the research, and at some point, we would have to look into doing some focus groups, that'll be important. Oh, and, of course, the information we gather is going to have to be analyzed." The same information is provided in both cases. However, the answer structured into digestible chunks offers that information with far greater clarity and precision. This not only makes it easier to understand, but also makes it easier to think about precise actions. Don't let your own knowledge of the material become a detriment to your ability to communicate what you know. Remember, it is likely that the listener in such a situation is hearing this information for the first time. Whenever you find yourself in one of these business conversations, and this applies to casual conversations as well, remember the key to effectively communicate what you know is to provide a bullet point structure that will make it easily digestible for the listener.

2. *Pauses:* Give your listeners strategically placed moments to gather their thoughts and refocus on what you're saying. This is the purpose of a pause. How and when do you pause? Pausing does not come naturally to us. Most of us are inclined to speak faster, and faster still if we can. The idea of pausing, therefore, seems counterintuitive. But again, such fast speaking will be a product of our enthusiasm and familiarity with the material we're discussing. In the consulting context though, it is highly likely that your listener is hearing this material for the first time. Digesting the material may be a challenge for them. Pauses can be extremely valuable in aiding assimilation of the new information. They serve as a kind of punctuation, providing a clear separation between the points. Verbally, it is the pause that makes an idea into a bullet point.

It is also important to make sure you are in fact providing a pause. Time passes in odd subjective ways inside your head, depending among other things, on how you're feeling about the situation (Eagleman, 2008). Sometimes we can feel like an eternity has passed when it's been a mere moment. At least in the beginning, make a conscious effort to be sure you've provided a sufficient pause. As long as two full seconds, is not too long. When I say "two seconds," you may think that's an awfully long time, but from the perspective of the listener, it's a comfortable amount of time to gather thoughts, integrate the information and still feel like the conversation is flowing at a productive pace. And, incidentally, don't underestimate the value of those pauses to you, the speaker. Those few seconds, while the listener is taking stock, you as the speaker can be organizing your next bullet point, considering how best to structure or word it. Again, this is something that requires conscious effort; it doesn't come naturally. With practice though, introducing pauses can become a powerful part of your business conversations.

3. *Hand gestures:* While delivering your response in a business conversation, making effective use of structured statements, punctuated with pauses, our communication can be further enhanced with the smart use of appropriate hand gestures. What kind of hand gesturing are we talking about, here? It could be as simple as using fingers to signify the number of points, counting them off on subsequent fingers, one by one. This, of course, helps the listener to further distinguish between the various bullet points. The goal of verbal bullet points is to be concise and focused. The punctuation of

pauses helps in providing these qualities; counting off on your fingers further emphasizes the structure, and isolates the points you want to press home in your conversation. The more such focused techniques you can use, the easier it is for the listener to zero in on your key points.

Let's review the BPSF. This is a framework for effectively presenting your ideas in bullet points. By chunking the content of your contributions to a conversation in such bullet points, you make it easier for the listener to understand your points and thereby, integrate or act on that information. This goal is achieved by providing a structure that organizes your thoughts into bullet points. Remember to not be shy, in the midst of a conversation, about politely asking for a moment to structure your response. This allows you the time to gather and organize your thoughts, and the listener will appreciate your efforts to be as explicit and systematic as possible. These can be very high stake conversations; it benefits both parties if the communication clarity can be maximized.

Once your structure is in place, it must be delivered effectively. An important part of that effective delivery is the judicious use of appropriate pauses. Pauses accentuate the various points, highlighting and distinguishing the discrete chunks of information you want to emphasize in your conversational reply. These pauses further contribute to the ease of the listener in focusing on your points, integrating the information, and thus making it a more actionable response. You can further provide this kind of emphasis and focus to your discrete points through the use of appropriate hand gestures. Counting off the points, each in turn, on the fingers of your hand is a classic set of gestures that can powerfully contribute to enhancing the effect of using bullet points. These are the keys to the BPSF: the bullet point speaking framework.

Body Language

The research of professor Albert Mehrabian, published in his book *Silent Messages*, reveals that as much as 93 percent of all communication is non-verbal (Mehrabian, 1972). The vast majority of what we communicate is in fact non-verbal. The breakdown of the 93 percent is also interesting for us. Body language is 55 percent of communication, with the other non-verbal 38 percent coming from inflection and tone of voice. The majority of all communication effect then comes from body language. Appreciating the incredible impact of body language is a huge factor in your ability to convey your messages for optimum benefit. Obviously, as I've emphasized in earlier parts of this book, choosing your words carefully is immensely important in communicating as a consultant. It turns out though that words are actually less influential than your body language. Understanding this can and should completely transform the way you look at your communication efforts and processes.

What is it that you need to be most aware of when considering the impact of your body language? This is, of course, an enormous topic, and there are many excellent books, including Mehrabian's, which you might consult to dive even deeper into this important and promising topic. For our purposes, here, I'll focus on three key aspects of the topic that I have found to be of great value.

1. *The Home Position* is the posture you come back to when

you're not using your hands or your body for a specific communication purpose. For example, if you observe people in a conversation, a standard home position, when not using hands or body for gesturing, is to sit with arms crossed over the chest. Sometimes people stand with their hands clasped in front or held behind their back. This might first seem like an obvious reset position when we're not using our hands or body to communicate. This assumption is mistaken though. Just because you're not using your body for a specific purpose doesn't mean that your body isn't still communicating something in the home position.

What is the most effective home position? This is what I call the open home position: you have your feet shoulder width apart or closer, but your hands are held by your side. Without a doubt, when you first think about creating this position, it might look awkward and even feel uncomfortable. The more common home positions express our defensive psychology from ancient times, where any stranger had to be considered a credible threat. In a truly dangerous situation, your disposition to protect your chest, say, with crossed arms, would be a smart choice. This evolved defensiveness though, is what evolutionary psychologists call a mismatch with the modern world. Unless you have reasons to suspect that your prospective client is going to plunge a spear into your chest, there's no actual need to defend your chest in such a way. And, in fact, operating entirely subconsciously, the client you're speaking to will pick up on the expression of trust and openness that your exposed chest communicates, promoting a connection between the two of you.

The home position should also be upright. Stand straight, with your shoulders wide and relaxed. This will allow you to look calm and composed, contributing further to the impression of being open and trustworthy. In contrast, an ineffective home posture is one that seems to close you off: arms crossed, hands clasped, leaning, slouching, etc. In all these positions, your primordial disposition to protect yourself around strangers is inducing a posture that in some way is blocking you off from the other person. These postures convey lack of trust and openness, subconsciously invoking a more cautious response from your conversational partner. These are not dynamics you want to trigger if you intend to be a legendary consultant.

2. *Pacifiers* is a concept I learned from a book called *The Power of Body Language* (Navarro, 2012). These are actions we engage in to calm ourselves. Obviously, we will be most prone to such actions when we are nervous. For instance, you'll notice many people, when giving public presentations will fidget with their hands. Some people will continually cap and uncap a marker pen. People will fiddle with their notebooks or shake their leg. Some will even bite their nails. These are all pacifiers. Such pacifiers are, of course, a natural technique that can be helpful in calming you in stressful situations. However, some of these pacifiers do not make a good impression on your audience. They're distracting and can convey feelings of underconfidence and possibly even incompetence. Effective communication requires you to be conscious of your own use of pacifiers. You want to make a deliberate and concerted effort to subdue such pacifiers

when engaged in conversations. Over time, your avoidance of such pacifiers will come to you as second nature.

3. *Eye contact* is the third aspect of body language I want to focus on, here. Intuitively, we all understand the importance of eye contact. If you've ever had a conversation, which I'm sure you have, with someone who wasn't looking at you during the discussion, and was instead looking down at the floor all the time, across the room or out the window, you've experienced that sense of being unappreciated, maybe even disrespected. You certainly come away from such an experience feeling that the person wasn't interested in you or what you had to say. Such an impression does nothing to build feelings of trust or confidence. You may think poorly of them, and are unlikely to have found the conversation productive. This is pretty much the opposite of how legendary consultants make their clients and colleagues feel.

You always want your clients to feel important when engaged in a business conversation with them. In truth, this priority shouldn't be limited to business conversations. Any time it is worth your while to have a conversation with another person, that person should feel that they were important to you. Making good eye contact is extremely important. However, it is also necessary to be aware of too much eye contact. You don't want to come off as compulsive or eccentric. Too much eye contact can feel invasive or even threatening. What then, is the most effective balance? My rule of thumb is that each time you make eye contact with someone, you should hold it for three to five seconds. Then look away for one to two seconds. This approach ensures sufficient eye contact to maintain a strong conversational connection, without crossing over the line into obsessive or uncomfortable interaction.

These are the three key aspects of body language that I would emphasize paying close attention to in your one-on-one business conversations, and indeed in your general conversation practices. Find a comfortable home position, which leaves you expressing feelings of openness and trustworthiness, with your shoulders relaxed and arms at your side. Identify and make a conscious effort to control and eventually eliminate your pacifiers. Develop the habit of making effective eye contact with your fellow conversationalist.

Listening

Listening is an incredibly important component of successful one-on-one business conversations. Great consultants, indeed great leaders, are great listeners. We have addressed this topic briefly in the chapters before, but here we want to dive deeper into it from the one-on-one conversation angle. Legendary consulting requires that you concentrate your efforts on building the skill of effective listening. And, have no doubt, it is a skill. You may think this is overblown; after all, we all listen to others all the time. But increasingly in the modern world, with all its distractions, we listen passively, even distractedly. What I'm emphasizing here is conscious, intentional listening. Renowned corporate executive advisor Bernard Ferrari calls this "power listening" (Ferrari, 2012).

Such focused listening does not come naturally to most of us. It is vitally important though. Listening is not merely an information gathering technique, it also communicates something about us to the speaker. Of course, listening with care allows you to better understand and assimilate what someone, say a client, is saying to you, but your intentional, focused listening also tells that client you're interested in what they have to say. It communicates that you care about them and value their experience and concerns. When people feel valued and appreciated, it increases their sense of self-worth, and they appreciate how you've contributed to those positive personal feelings. This dynamic is exceptionally important in developing a strong, trusting relationship with clients or anyone else you deal with in your business life. The question becomes, how can you be sure you are listening effectively and conveying that fact to others? Here are some valuable suggestions:

1. Convey appropriate verbal and non-verbal signals. Verbal signals can be non-linguistic sounds which you make to indicate you're hearing and understanding what is being said. The standard "hmm" or "uh-huh." They can also be linguistics sounds, like "yes" or "I see." Non-verbal signals can include posture, gestures, facial expressions, eye contact, etc. - any signal that indicates attentiveness and interest.

2. It is critical to confirm what you've heard. After the client has finished speaking, provide a brief summary of what was said as a way of demonstrating that you were listening attentively. This has an additional benefit of clarifying what they said. If your summary resonates with the client's

intention, this will be a valuable marker, allowing you to move on to the next point. However, not all clients are necessarily great communicators, and your summary may help the client realize that they didn't say what they wanted to say, or not in the way they had intended. This provides an opportunity for them to restate it and ensure increased clarity as the conversation moves forward. Clarifying your own perspective is useful. You can begin with something along the lines of: "Okay, so, what I heard was..." or "so, what you're looking for is..." This is powerful stuff: practices that you'll find highly refined among the top one percent of consultants.

3. Silence is also a vitally important dimension of listening. Silence shows confidence. In the modern world though, people are increasingly uncomfortable with silence. There's a perceived obligation to fill any silence with some small talk, something witty or intelligent, or even just some prattle. This is a misguided impulse. It is important that you become comfortable with silence. When you have nothing important or meaningful to say, it is better to not say anything. Two benefits come from such a comfort with silence. First, it allows us to be better listeners, as it provides the speaker time to gather or refine their thoughts. Second, if we're not constantly saying inane things, when we do speak, the value of what we have to say is enhanced. It's analogous to supply and demand: the person of few words gets a lot more attention when they say those few words. Clients value their time, and they'll appreciate you showing that you value it too by not wasting it with inane prattle. Make your words

count. Being comfortable with silence allows you to do so.

We've identified three valuable techniques to exercise the kind of effective listening that enhances our business conversations. These were, using verbal and non-verbal signals to convey your interest in and attentiveness to your clients or other conversational partners. Intermittently confirming what the other person said ensures that both partners in the conversation are understanding each other as they progress in the discussion. Finally, becoming comfortable with silence allows your conversational partner the optimum opportunity to gather their thoughts and express their ideas, while also investing more value in what you have to say, provided you choose your words judiciously, rather than succumbing to the temptation to fill in the silence with empty chatter.

This brings us to the final topic under the rubric of one-on-one business conversations: giving feedback.

Giving Feedback

Giving feedback is one of life's most critical skills and aptitudes. It's essential to provide effective feedback to everyone in your life: clients, partners, spouses, children, etc. Great consultants and leaders are able to provide feedback effectively. Let's look at how this is done. To start, you have to know why you're offering feedback. The underlying purpose of all feedback is to provide someone the ability to see something about themselves, which they had previously been unable to see, so that that person can perform better in the future. You're trying to help them improve their performance (Pozen, 2013). A part of this, of course, is simply telling someone what they can do differently and possibly pointing out the potential benefits of doing so. Great feedback though, goes beyond this. It doesn't merely instruct, it also inspires.

To help someone get the best out of themselves, you want to motivate them. You don't want them receiving your feedback as negative criticism or fault-finding; you want them to feel excited about the opportunity that your feedback allows them to succeed in some area in which they had previously struggled. This will encourage them to raise their game and try harder. It is important to put the emphasis on what's possible in the future, rather than what failed in the past. Just as important as what can be improved, is appreciating what has already been done well. We want to build on prior successes, not throw the baby out with the bathwater.

Acknowledging what was done well in the past is an important part of building the encouragement that inspires future aspirations. Good feedback always starts with appreciation. The feedback is an opportunity to benefit and improve going forward. Use terms like opportunity, benefit, potential, etc. A positive tone is always more inspiring. As popular science writer Annie Murphy Paul emphasizes, a consideration for effective feedback is the importance of being specific (Paul, 2013). For instance, when accentuating the positive: it's not enough to tell someone that some aspect of what they did was great. It's important to identify precisely what was great in what they did and why you value it. If you're providing feedback on a presentation that had a lot of problems, but the introduction was good. Of course, start there, but it's not nearly as helpful to just say, "Oh, you began well." What was good about the beginning: was the topic introduced in a compelling way? Did the introduction provide a thorough overview of the topics to be discussed? Did it succeed in making a potentially dry topic seem accessible and exciting? Whatever it was about the start of the presentation that was good, this is what needs to be communicated. It provides something tangible to be proud of and to build upon going forward.

Another important aspect of effective feedback, which doesn't always get the attention it deserves, is presenting new opportunities with a clear demonstration. After all, while there's opportunity for greater benefits in the future by doing something differently, if the receiver of the feedback has no idea what they could do differently, such opportunities might seem vague, maybe even illusionary. I mean, if they knew how to do it better, they probably would have done it better. Rather than merely stating that the data analysis presentation could be better, provide a brief demonstration of how it could be better: maybe a different visual display could be used. Perhaps color-coding of curves on a graph would highlight key points more effectively. Possibly a bar chart would be more effective than a line graph for this particular data display. Something concrete to demonstrate the opportunities always provides for more effective feedback.

The best feedback is rooted in an appreciation of the person. It requires a positive outlook and a specific focus on opportunities. This approach increases the likelihood that the person receiving the feedback is inspired to improve their performance going forward.

This wraps up the discussion of one-on-one business conversation as a part of the communication mastery dimension of the legendary consulting system. We've emphasized the importance of body language and listening as means of building trust and confidence within your conversational partner. This approach creates valuable relationships while providing the most effective grounds for mutual understanding and clarity of intention as the two of you move through the phases of your professional association. Sometimes giving feedback will be an aspect of business conversations. An upbeat and tangible approach provides the best outcomes for all involved. Employing these insights will help you achieve the kind of business conversations that characterize the practices of the legendary consulting system.

We're now ready to move on to the next topic in this chapter: presentation skills and public speaking.

Presentation Skills and Speaking

Most consultants, on a regular basis, have to deliver presentations in front of a gathering of people. You may have to present your proposals, your findings or your recommendations. Plus, there's often a selling component to this: you're selling your ideas for new paths or follow-up projects. Influencing others, clients or teams is usually an important part of such presentations. All of this, then, means that effective public speaking is going to be critical to your success as a consultant. Mastering these skills is essential to being a legendary consultant.

Public speaking is a set of skills that improves with practice. All the skills and tips I'll be providing for you in this section will only benefit you if you can take that next step and start to implement, i.e. practice your public speaking. You'll want to begin doing so in a safe environment.

Rehearsal is essential. Most good public speakers rehearse before they deliver a speech in public. This cannot be overstated.

You might consider joining your local Toastmasters International chapter to provide yourself the right kind of safe, encouraging, supportive atmosphere to conduct your practicing. Toastmasters has played an enormous role in my consulting career, allowing me to take it and even my life to a new level. I always recommend Toastmasters to anyone who wants to improve their public speaking and leadership skills or just simply grow as a person.

When pondering over the prospects of providing a presentation in any given consulting context, the very first question I would recommend that you pose to yourself is this: "Do I really need to do such a presentation?" Does the information you want to convey actually need to be presented publicly or will an email be sufficient to cover the topic, in the form of a memo? Consider whether a back-and-forth will be required to optimize the information. Is there a potential for misunderstanding in a memo? If that's the case, then certainly a presentation makes sense. However, if not, you don't need a public presentation, and it would be wiser to not unnecessarily use the time of those involved. So when considering your options and requirements, this should always be the first question: "Is this prospective presentation actually necessary?"

If the answer is yes, then there are some considerations you can take account of for the optimum benefit from your presentations. The areas I'll examine are the following: structure, PowerPoint tips, and delivery.

Structure

At the highest level, a public presentation should be structured into three clearly delineated parts: the opening, the body, and the conclusion. Let's look at what's important in each of these:

1. *The opening* of your presentation should, first, grip your audience. You want to hook them in so that they're keen to hear the rest of what you have to say. This is a critical outcome that you want to achieve in the first 60 seconds of your presentation. The opening also needs to clearly define the purpose of your presentation. What will the listeners learn by paying attention to what you have to say? And, what are the actionable outcome that you want to achieve with this presentation? For instance, if there's a decision that you want to be made as a result of your presentation, make sure to explicitly highlight that in your opening. Or if it's a findings sharing or a status update and next steps review, whatever the purpose of the presentation, make sure its goals are clearly stated. Provide a clear statement of the presentation's purpose and do so in a way that captures and holds the audience's attention. And, again, this should be done in the first 60 seconds; that's what you should consider as your opening. Let's consider some opening strategies:

    i. You could start by showcasing an *interesting statistic*. The statistic should be striking, even surprising. This will encourage the audience to know the story behind it and be motivated to concentrate on your presentation. For example: "The total energy required to run the world for a year, is equal to one day of solar energy."

This opening is not only interesting but also pushes the audience to think a certain way. Needless to say, we need to be sure that our statistic ties into the rest of our presentation.

ii. Open with a *question*. This strategy is good because it starts a conversation. Questions are conversational by their very nature. Invoking such a conversation motivates your audience to attend your presentation as though they were going to provide you a response, even if your question is only rhetorical. There's an additional benefit to asking a non-rhetorical question, as it takes the immediate attention and pressure off the speaker, by putting the spotlight, for the moment at least, on those answering the question. After a few people have offered different answers, the audience will now be additionally motivated to find out from you which of the different solutions, in fact, is correct.

iii. Often it's good to follow these initial attention grabbers with a *story*, something autobiographical, which will provide a concrete illustration of the broader point you want to make in your presentation. Or you can start directly with the story. Think about the story with which I started this book, about my family driving our cherry red Maruti Suzuki 800 on a foggy winter day in India. Humans are storytelling animals; we get caught up in narratives (Sugiyama, 1996). If you choose the right story, something compelling in its own right, but tailored to dovetail effectively with the core theme of your presentation, this is a powerful way of hooking your audience. Maybe you could choose to describe your experience at a store, or your experience of buying something online, or how you solved a particular problem you were facing; stories are powerful.

iv. A precise *map* of the presentation should be a part of the opening. Spell out how the information is structured and in what order the audience can expect to go through your assessment. Perhaps you will start by stating a problem or challenge; then you'll look at the data relevant to this situation; then you'll conclude with an evidence-based recommendation. Something along these lines; whatever is appropriate for the specific context of your presentation.

v. Finally, the outcome has to *make explicit the purpose* of the presentation: what is your intended outcome? No matter what it is: to lay out a clear plan; establish various roles and responsibilities within the team; make a decision on contractor hiring, etc. your presentation won't be worth taking up the time of everyone involved unless it has a tangible purpose. Be sure that your opening spells that out to make everyone clear about what's at stake.

2. *The body* of the presentation comes next. The body is where the substance of the material is presented. It's the main attraction: why we're all here. What then, constitutes a well-structured presentation?

The primary consideration for effective body construction, going back to our earlier discussion of business conversation structure, is the use of bullet points. If you think about structuring your presentation into bullet points, you'll be off on the right foot in terms of organizing your thoughts around key chunks of information. I suggest dividing your body into 3 to 5 components or bullet points.

Using bullet points also makes it easier to convey your ideas to the audience, who is consequently better able to sort those ideas in their own minds and better prepare for the flow of the argument you are making.

3. *The closing* pulls it all together for your audience. Its key components will be a review, a conclusion and a look toward next steps.

   i. If it's a one-sided presentation, you will want to *review the key findings and analyses*. If the process was more conversational, and especially if some important decision was made, the review will recap the central themes of the discussion and reiterate the decisions, so that everyone is on the same page moving forward.

   ii. The conclusion allows a *restatement of core decisions or insights* arising from the presentation, and, in a consulting context specifically, the conclusion should put any such decisions or insights into the larger context of the project's progress. What impact does the discussion or decisions today have on the nature, pace or direction of the overall project? Everyone needs to be clear and, again, on the same page about these impacts.

   iii. That leads us directly into the *next steps*. If the results of the presentation are a change in the nature, pace or direction of the larger project, how are these changes to be implemented? Ultimately, resolving that question might be another presentation or discussion of its own, but at the very least it needs to be made explicit that putting into action today's decisions or insights will require concrete steps. If they can be spelled out today, in this presentation, that should be done so that action can be initiated.

Your presentation requires an opening that captures the attention of the audience and informs them of the steps you'll be following in the course of your presentation. The purpose of the presentation needs to be highlighted in the opening. The main body of that presentation needs to be broken up into clearly delineated, step by step units that are both easy to follow and that organize the material into a logical and clear format. This can be achieved by presenting the body in discrete bullet points. In the closing, whatever decisions or insights arose from the presentation need to be reviewed. Then the conclusion puts the lessons learned or decisions made into the broader context of the overall project. The next steps, the final part of the closing, looks at how to implement the appropriate changes to the nature, pace or direction of the larger project.

PowerPoint

The PowerPoint presentation has become the professional standard for business presentations, today. It is essential that PowerPoint is efficiently used; as leadership development consultant Kristi Hedges observes, PowerPoint misuse is actually counterproductive and can harm your presentation (Hedges, 2014). Here are some valuable tips for making your PowerPoint presentations as effective and powerful as possible:

1. The PowerPoint presentation is a tool for conveying information effectively and efficiently. Like with any tool, experience and knowledge can increase your proficiency in its operation. This tool is one that provides us a tremendous range of features. Judiciously used, these features can help really emphasize or clarify a point. There is a danger though, in getting too caught up in all the bells and whistles. Adding animation or transitions that are not driven by an informational need all too often wind up being distracting, actually undermining the successful communication of your message. McKinsey and Co., a world-leading consulting firm, is noteworthy for their use of a very plain, stripped down PowerPoint formatting style. Their goal is to keep the attention focused on the core message. Too many bells and whistles distract from that end. This is an insight you should bring to your own PowerPoint presentations.

2. The *rule of 10-20-30*. This is a rule I've coined for optimum PowerPoint effectiveness. This is a rule of thumb for how to organize your presentation: you need 10 slides, with a minimum 20-point font, for your 30-minute presentation. The average length of a business presentation is around 30 minutes, so generally we'll be aiming for that. Given that time frame, 10 slides provide you the appropriate amount of content to easily and comfortably cover in that period of time. The 20-point font limit is a valuable internal check

against the danger, which we all are inclined toward, of trying to squeeze too much content onto any one slide. The 10 slide rule won't be much help in regulating an appropriate amount of content for your 30-minute presentation if you're cramming an unwieldy amount of text into those slides.

3. Emphasize *visually presented information.* If you have data to show, do so on a line graph or on a bar or pie chart. With a little imagination, you might be surprised how much information you can convey visually if you set your mind to it. Your audience will find it far easier and faster to comprehend and process information that is presented to them visually.

To summarize, keep your PowerPoint animations and fancy transitions to a minimum: you want to emphasize the information, not startle the audience with your technical wizardry. Follow the 10-20-30 rule, by using only 10 slides, with a minimum of 20-point font, when preparing a 30-minute presentation. And always try to embellish the information in your presentation through some visual display. Following these three tips will help your audience to stay attentive, focused on your key message, and quickly and easily absorb the information you're presenting.

Delivery

Everything we've discussed about public speaking and presentation has been focused on making your presentation as effective as possible. Nothing is more important in achieving that end than ensuring that your delivery is also as effective as possible.

5 - Communication Skills Mastery

Consider these aspects for excellent delivery of your public presentations:

1. *Get to the point.* And do it quickly. This is a critically important part of presentation delivery, which is the Achilles' heel of too many consultants. Too often, too many start off with some kind of small talk, commenting on the weather, or the ordeal of their commute that morning, etc. It dilutes the impact. We all get enough small talk during the day. You've brought these people here for a reason, respect their time, and be aware of everyone's attention limits. Get to the point. It will present you as focused and purposeful.

2. *Eye contact* was already discussed in the section on one-on-one conversations; it is no less important in public presentations. A sure way to lose your audience is to read from the screen or prepared text, or to gaze at the floor or the ceiling. This will not effectively engage your audience. Don't just speak to a crowd, speak to individuals in that crowd. It will actually benefit you: when you make eye contact with people, the human connection will lead them to offer body language cues, like nodding or smiling, in acknowledgment of what you're saying, and you can feed off this input. Furthermore, it engages them, drawing them into the world you're creating at center stage. They'll much more readily enter the world of your presentation if you invite them in personally through your eye contact.

3. *Stage position* is a consideration of where you're standing during your presentation. The best place to stand is at the left of the screen as seen from the audience's perspective. At

least, this is true for any cultures with languages, like English, where people read left to right. When the right side of a page is reached, we automatically jump all the way back to the left side of the page. It's a subconscious, automatic reset point. If you're situated at the left side of the screen, it is a smooth transition for the audience to move from the presenter, to read a sentence off the screen, then naturally return to the presenter. Standing to the right of the screen disrupts this smooth flow and creates an awkward presentation, which can distract from the presentation's content.

4. *Proximity* is another dimension of stage positioning. How far are you from the audience? This subconsciously conveys information to the audience about your own confidence. Proximity conveys certainty. The closer you are to your audience the easier it is for them to feel your energy and thereby the more confident you seem. Coming across as energetic and confident goes a long way in being able to sell your ideas and influence your audience. Of course, you don't want to invade the personal space of anyone in the audience, but a good general rule is to always try to be decently close to them while you're presenting.

5. *Body movement* should be limited on stage. A lot of presenters tend to pace across the stage. This is not an optimum presentation strategy (N. Robbins, 2012). All body movement should be purposeful. If there isn't a presentation-related reason for moving your body, you shouldn't move it.

6. *Less is more!* This reprises our 10-20-30 rule. Do not overdo it. Do not try to speak too much. Do not try to present too much information. The judicious parsing of what you need

to say allows what you do say to be most effective because it's not being lost in a sea of extraneous words and ideas. Identify your key point and stick to it. This is the most direct route to audience clarity and client action. And that's what your presentation is all about.

These are our six best practices for public presentation delivery. Get to the point, quickly. No small talk and chit-chat. Make eye contact, turn the crowd into a group of individuals, who you engage personally with and draw into your presentation. Be aware of your stage position: stand to the audience's left of your PowerPoint screen and maintain a powerful proximity with the audience by stepping toward them as you make important points. Limit your body movement so as not to distract your audience. Be sure that any body movements you do make are harnessed toward emphasizing something important in the presentation. And, remember, overloading your audience with information is counterproductive; follow the time-worn dictum: less is more.

If you follow the guidelines in this section, you'll be on your way to making effective and powerful presentations, through successful public speaking occasions. Structure your presentation with an effective opening, body, and closing. Use PowerPoint, but be sure to use it effectively and not lapse into the traps that make it counterproductive for some presenters. Keep it focused and ensure the features you use have an informational purpose. Finally, pay attention to your presentation delivery: including body language and positioning. Your best public presentation will be the one in which you get to the point and stay on the point. People are sacrificing their valuable time to hear your presentation; it is your job to ensure that it is the best possible use of their time. They'll best benefit this way from the value you can add to their business with your presentation, and they'll appreciate your respect for their time and attention.

Leading Effective Meetings

Nowadays meetings come in different and surprising forms. We're all familiar with the traditional idea of a meeting in which people gather in a single room, around a table, to deal with the issues they need to resolve. This is the old roundtable version of the meeting. However, over recent years, it has become increasingly common to hold business meetings in which many of the attendees, are in completely different rooms, possibly spread out over the world. These are what might be called virtual meetings. They rely on several telecommunication methods, from telephone to Skype, to state of the art online teleconferencing technologies. While there are a wide range of common strategies that are crucial for effective leadership of such meetings, of both kinds. In this section, we will be addressing these core, common strategies for leading effective meetings.

Leading meetings effectively is important for consultants who are often working under tight deadlines and across different units. Ensuring that responsibilities are clearly delineated and acknowledged, while also expediting decision-making processes, is optimized by effective meeting planning and execution. The legendary consultants, the top one percent, are those who are able to keep their meetings focused, on track and goal-oriented.

The first step in dealing with meetings, as was the case with presentations, is asking yourself if, in fact, you do need the meeting. Perhaps the issue can be addressed through email, copying and soliciting the input of the appropriate parties. Elizabeth Grace Saunders offers a helpful decision tree that you can consult for determining whether a meeting is really needed (Saunders, 2015). If the answer to that question is yes, you'll need to know how to get the most out of the limited time others have put aside to meet with you. We will look at the strategies to achieve that end:

1. *Circulate the agenda.* If you know that you need the meeting, you know what you need to discuss. Put that down in an agenda which you can send to the participants in advance, so they have enough time to review it and prepare for the meeting. As a part of the agenda, break down the tasks and time allocated for each of those tasks.

2. *Ensure the right people are present.* An important part of this strategy involves an awareness of the misalignments of perspective within the client company. It's not uncommon for different departments or organizational teams to have different preferences and priorities. Sometimes it is valuable to iron out such differences, but other times it simply isn't worth wasting time on listening to them repeat longstanding differences. It is important for you to know about the existence of such divisions, what the grounds of their differences are, and decide what is a better use of everyone's time, whether these differences need to be resolved or simply planned around with multiple meetings. Appropriate decision makers are also important considerations. If you'll want an organizational commitment for a decision mov-

ing forward, there's no point holding a meeting to get that commitment unless the appropriate decision-makers, who can put the decision into operation, are present. Whatever the consideration, be sure everyone you need is present, and that anyone who is extraneous to the meeting's purpose is absent.

3. *Align your appearance.* Dressing the part is crucial. As we've discussed, attention to appearance is always important for the consultant, but that is never truer than when you're leading a meeting. Research has shown the impact dress choices have on those around us (O'Neal & Lapitsky, 1991). If you're dressed the part, there'll be greater buy-in of you as a leader, with a subsequently greater willingness to follow your lead. Your recommendations are much more likely to be positively greeted. As a consequence, you are much more likely to successfully achieve your desired ends. Dress the part. For suggestions on how to do so, have a look at Kim Lachance Shandrow's article in *Entrepreneur* (Shandrow, 2014).

4. *Clearly communicate the intended outcome.* Before calling a meeting, you must be clear about what it is that you want to achieve, and that purpose needs to be communicated to the participants. Again, this dovetails the discussion above on presentations. You're taking up other people's time, you have a specific purpose, and probably a limited window of opportunity to achieve that purpose. Getting everyone as focused as possible, right from the start, is your best bet for success. Clearly, communicate the outcome you intend to achieve in the meeting. Occasionally, openly stating the end goal explicitly from the start may stir up some

resistance; in such a case, it may be necessary to allow the evidence to accumulate from the meeting's proceedings. Early communication in those rare cases may be counterproductive, but even in those situations, it is still essential that you know the purpose of the meeting and the outcome you intend to achieve.

5. *Have a supporter.* There are a variety of activities which may come up in the course of a meeting: for example, note-taking, brainstorming ideas, flipping charts. Of course, you can do this yourself, but your meeting is going to be more effective if you can concentrate your time and effort on dealing with the intellectual content and the group dynamic. Having someone along to support you in conducting the meeting, to free you of such tasks, allows you to focus your energy on the most important aspects of the meeting.

6. *Focus.* A successful meeting is a result of the meeting leader keeping the meeting on track. Humans are a congenial bunch, and most of them enjoy talking. There's usually no malicious intent involved; it's just that one thing suggests another, and then another still: next thing you know an engaging discussion is taking place that unfortunately has nothing to do with the intended outcome of the meeting. No matter how much the participants might be enjoying the tangent, the fact is that they are wasting time by not focusing on the topic of the meeting. It is the meeting leader's job to protect the participants from wasting time and squandering this opportunity to resolve important issues. Some leash, of course, must be extended. It's possible a wrinkle in the situation you hadn't considered has been

discovered in the collective wisdom of the group. If you've properly prepared, this is not likely, but it can happen. You don't want to rashly shut down avenues of discussion which might prove unexpectedly fruitful. At the end of the day, even in that situation, the meeting still has an intended outcome, and as the leader, your job is to always get the focus back to addressing that issue.

7. *Keep track of time*: This point aligns closely with the point above. It is important that you at all times are aware of how your meeting is performing in relation to the time allocated. If you are not on track to achieving the intended outcome in the set time, it is your responsibility to change gears and do what you can to make the meeting a success. The general formula that works to keep track of time is 20-50-30. This formula suggests that in a typical meeting which could be anywhere from 30 minutes to 90 minutes long, you should spend about 20% of the time for the introduction. This involves giving all the attendees the background on why the meeting is scheduled, what the intended outcome is and how they can contribute. This component can involve a formal presentation. Next, 50% of the time should be spent on discussion and planning. This could involve group brainstorming, gathering creative ideas or making decisions on the main topic. Finally, the last 30% of the meeting should be spent on summarizing the discussion, establishing consensus and briefly planning the next steps.

This simple formula 20-50-30 helps you to ensure that meeting is on track with clear outcomes that you should have achieved at any point in the meeting.

8. *Follow-up.* A best practice in ensuring an effective follow-up is to send a group email to everyone who attended the meeting listing the "next steps" that were identified and agreed upon in the meeting. Roles and responsibilities should be reiterated.

Following these eight strategies will help you lead effective meetings, whether those meetings are around a table or around the world. Always start off by asking whether you actually need a meeting, or will some other medium, such as a group email, be a more efficient use of your and everyone else's time. If you do need a meeting, be clear about what you want to accomplish and how to accomplish that purpose during the meeting. Answering these questions will allow you to send an advance copy of the meeting agenda, breaking it down into its functional parts so that the meeting participants are up to speed and ready to go right from the start. Answering these questions also allows you to have a clear picture in your own mind about what the intended outcome is. And, when appropriate, you are better able to express those intentions from the start, so everyone has a sense of a common purpose. Make sure to have the right people in the room: everyone who needs to be there is, anyone who doesn't need to be there isn't. Also, remember to dress the part of the meeting leader; dressing appropriately can significantly affect your meeting's outcome. Have a supporter to help you with ordinary tasks so that you can concentrate your energy on the intellectual content and group dynamic. Keep the meeting on track so that the time allotted for the meeting isn't squandered and your project goals can be advanced. Finally, reinforce the outcome of the meeting with a follow-up email that reviews decisions made and reminds every one of the roles and responsibilities established in the meeting.

Email and Phone Communication

We are living in a world in which the fabric of our communicational life is increasingly woven out of email and phone correspondence. These communication methods are undoubtedly central to the organizational life of our clients. They are probably receiving hundreds of emails daily. Likewise, depending on the nature of their business, they may well be inundated daily with telephone calls. This is the sea of modern communication within which we all must swim. The legendary consultants distinguish themselves by their adept navigation of these turbulent waters. The ability to operate effectively in this world of email and phone calls is only going to become of ever greater premium. There are more multi-location teams today than ever in the past. The trend lines all point toward the continued growth of such organizational practices. The legendary consultant is the one who swims in this virtual communicational world like a fish in water.

Pros and Cons of Different Communication Media

Let's continue with a discussion of what media are available to you and how to identify which is the right one for any particular purpose. An extremely important medium is *face-to-face communication*. This medium promotes clarity through transparency. Eye contact and body language are easily observed, which, as we've discussed above, contribute to higher levels of trust and confidence. This is an especially valuable medium for dealing with emotional communication. Where emotions are at stake, the high trust level provides significant value. On the downside, such face-to-face meetings do tend to be less efficient. They invariably involve some degree of travel, which is an inconvenience within the same city, and an increasingly larger one between cities. Also, both parties, to varying degrees, may have to reorganize their schedules to accommodate the meeting. Another potential drawback in face-to-face communication arises when it takes place in a meeting setting, where one person is addressing several others. This communication medium presents the danger of the discussion deteriorating into a one-sided monologue. The back-and-forth that makes communication a rich co-germination of ideas is lost in such situations. Here the key benefit of face-to-face interactions is self-defeated.

The next medium to consider is *phone communication*. Phone communication avoids the pitfalls associated with travel that we discussed as a part of the face-to-face interaction. These days most people have phones readily at hand, so there's much less inconvenience and inefficient time use involved. Yet, phones provide the same back-and-forth conversational opportunity that make the face-to-face meetings particularly effective. New ideas and insights can be built through conversation. Thanks to being able to hear each other's voice, there is still some capacity to communicate and read emotions, though of course, visual cues are absent. Phone communication can be much more spontaneous, not requiring a long lead time or scheduled plan to quickly have a discussion to deal with a pressing concern. On the other side, without a scheduled plan for the conversation, it isn't always possible to reach people by phone. Busy people often have their phones set to voicemail. It turns out in practice that scheduling a call often is the best idea, anyway. Also, while phone communication can be used for group meetings, they are less effective. When meetings start having 10 or 15 participants, the phone conference can become unmanageable.

The other medium widely used in the business world today is *email communication*. Indeed, this is probably the most commonly used communication medium in today's business world. Email is efficient and instantaneous. Everyone in the chain of communication is able to contribute to the discussion at their earliest convenience. No coordination is required beyond that. Email is very good for status updates, where no back-and-forth communication is required. It has the convenience of being able to send electronic files. Also, email scales well: one single email can be drafted to communicate with a single individual or a team. Email is useful for establishing an electronic record of the correspondence so that the parties can refer back to clarify the terms of prior discussions and decisions. However, it is less effective when multiple parties are trying to hammer out an agreement through a series of exchanges. Even keeping track of all the points made in the numerous emails of a single thread can be challenging after the exchange starts leading into dozens of individual messages. If side threads start sprouting, the problem can become entirely uncontrollable. And, of course, when a quick reply is needed for a pressing concern, email can be frustratingly slow in generating the needed discussion and agreement. It can be hours or, in some circumstances, even days to get a reply.

Which Communication Medium Should You Choose?

Deciding which communication medium is best to use in any circumstance requires clearly identifying the outcome you're trying to achieve. As we've seen, if you're only providing a status update, email would be the best choice. If your communication must make a decision, which requires some back-and-forth and clarification of terms and ideas along the way, involving say upwards of four or five people, that's probably going to be best achieved through a face-to-face meeting. This assumes it is feasible and cost-effective for those people to gather in the same location in a timely manner. If it turns out that the cost or inconvenience is too great for such a gathering, your best back up plan will be using the phone. As we've seen, there are certain qualities of each of the main communication media, and you should consider the pros and cons of each when deciding which communication medium to use.

However, there is another consideration that you should keep in mind. If there's ever any doubt in your mind about the optimum medium choice based on that medium's communicational qualities, it is always best to play to your own strength. We all have different strengths. Some of us are particularly gifted writers, others have the gift of the gab and are most effective in interpersonal communication, such as in a face-to-face context. Unless there is a clear and unambiguous set of criteria leading you to choose one communication medium over another, which often there is not, in that case, choose the medium that allows you to make the most of your own strengths, and thereby provide the best value to your clients.

Strategies for Effective Email Communication

Email is ubiquitous in our world. We're all constantly under a deluge and the pressures to get through them can create counter-incentives for optimal email practices. This situation leaves many people appearing frivolous as a consequence of imprecise or excessively casual email use. Such an outcome can be reinforced by the fact that email leaves a permanent electronic record. Consequently, caution and cognizance of these prospects need to inform your use of this communication medium. Let's look at some strategies that will help you produce more effective emails, which will reflect well on you:

1. *Know your audience.* Know their skill level. How familiar are they with the topic you are addressing in the email? Nothing productive comes from providing people with information which they're unable to assess. An audience that isn't math savvy will profit little from an email packed with statistical analysis. You're going to have to spell it out for them in words.

2. *Know your purpose.* What do you want to achieve with this particular email? Is it a status update, an approval request, a question, a funding request? You won't be able to write an effective email unless you know why you're writing it. Successfully achieving that goal will be most enhanced by keeping your focus on a single purpose. Don't muddy the water with multiple purposes.

3. *Be polite.* And, in fact, this advice might be extended to being diplomatic. It's not enough to simply avoid cursing and being inappropriately familiar. Those things are required

too, but consider the subtly of your wording. Remember, any time you ask anyone to do something for you, you're asking them to make a sacrifice of their time, energy or attention. Remember that and never allow your wording to suggest you feel entitled to their time, energy or attention. Don't tell someone what you need, instead ask if they can help you solve your problem.

4. *Be positive.* Use upbeat words like "opportunity," "growth," and "improvement." Consultants are brought in to make things better. A positive attitude is the first big step in ensuring things do get better, so make sure the language you use is a harbinger of that positive attitude.

5. *Be concise and brief.* In the writing of email, the rule of thumb is that brevity is strength. And that brevity is in your own interest. You may feel in the short run you're sacrificing saying everything you'd like to say on behalf of your case, but the more concise your email, the easier it is for the reader to consume and digest it. That ease on the part of the reader, in the long run, increases the likelihood of you receiving a prompt response. This is another classic case of the old saying: less is more.

6. *Use formatting.* Don't be shy about using underlining, *italics* or **bold** font to provide the emphasis necessary to convey your message as concisely and clearly as possible. And, of course, we've already talked at length about the value of bullet points. All these formatting devices provide graphic dimensions to your text. And you know how many words they say that a picture is worth. Judicious use of formatting gives your email that stronger visual component. The better

the reader understands what you're saying, the more likely they are to act on your suggestion. Using the visual cues of formatting to organize the presentation of your ideas will greatly facilitate the reader's understanding.

7. *Write effective subject lines.* This is so important yet so easily overlooked. Remember, for many people the subject line of your email is not only the first thing they see but in some cases, it could very well be the only thing they see. You want to grab your reader's attention and convince them to open your message. Even in situations, where they're obliged to open it, there are things you can do to promote more timely and appropriate responses to your email. Consider something simple. Rather than this: "Re: Phase Two of Project X." Try something like this: "[Phase Two, Project X] Questions for You." The first reads like another dull email on one of several projects that could be crossing the reader's desk. The second option addresses the reader specifically: "I have questions that only you can answer." This approach stirs feelings of responsibility and prestige. The reader has an important role to play, and others are depending on them to rise to the occasion. Another strategy, going in a different direction, is to use the subject line: "Quick Question." This makes your email sound casual and contributes to the reader feeling like there is less pressure for a response. Consequently, you can usually expect a faster turnaround. This casual approach, of course, has to be built on a level of familiarity established over time with the other person.

These are seven valuable strategies to employ when bringing your email writing up to the level of the legendary consultants. Know your audience, what they know and how to address them. Know your purpose and be brief and concise in your email writing, so that you can be laser focused on getting to the point and ensuring the most effective reply. Be polite, diplomatic and positive: attitude means a lot in any relationship, but having the right attitude is vital to effective consulting. Remember, your email remains an electronic record that can be consulted in the future. You want your professionalism to be your lasting legacy on that record. Use formatting to accentuate your key points so that you can increase the reader's comprehension and improve the prospect of prompt and effective follow-up on your email. And, remember, your subject line is the first impression of any email you send. Don't let it be the last. Use lines that stir the reader to action; that inspire interest and commitment.

Strategies for Effective Phone Communication

As we've discussed, there are many business communications that require a back-and-forth process to be effective in a timely manner. However, nowadays, with our globally connected markets and indeed just living in massive cities as so many of us now do, face-to-face meeting opportunities are limited by the high cost of travel. Alongside the tremendous innovations in mobile phone technology, phone communication has become increasingly important over the decades. Today's successful consultant has to be able to make effective use of this communication medium. As with writing emails, there are strategies you can follow as a consultant to get the most out of phone communications:

Get advance agreement. How many times have you had someone call you at just the wrong time? If you're not yet convinced you want to even talk to this person, the poor timing can be enough to leave a bad taste and put you off wanting to have the conversation later. And even if it is someone to whom you wish to speak, the awkwardness of having to put them off can be uncomfortable for all involved. You don't want to be put in those situations, so don't do it to others. If there's enough lead time, you can send an advance email to schedule a phone conversation. This can be done with secretaries or assistants, as well. And if you find yourself directly on the line with someone, in an unscheduled call, after exchanging brief pleasantries, before getting into your reason for calling, be sure to ask whether this is a convenient time, or if there is a better time you can call back? When asking if it's convenient, it helps the other person assess the situation better if you can provide an estimate of the time you anticipate taking up. If you think the call will need five to seven minutes, tell them that. And, in doing this, be specific and realistic. If you misjudge the time, which can happen to anyone, be sure to check again, after the estimated time has elapsed: "I know I said five to seven minutes, but it seems like this matter may take longer. Are you okay to continue or should I call back at a more convenient time?" This shows respect for the person you're talking to and demonstrates that you're reasonable. The overall result is that you'll be seen as a professional.

1. *Open with the main intent of the call.* You shouldn't be calling this person and taking up their time unless you know precisely why you're calling. If you do, don't beat around the bush. Respect their time. Tell them exactly why you're calling so the time you've scheduled, whether previously or at the beginning of the call, is put to the best use in both of your interests.

2. *Be concise and crisp.* I had mentioned the importance of being concise in the discussion of email strategies; this is even more important for phone communication. Unlike email, the person on the other end of the phone will not have the opportunity to review your conversation. They'll hear what you have to say only once, so you want your message to be as relevant and on target as possible. Get to the point.

3. *Show them the map.* If you've initiated this call, its success is up to you. Even if you've called the other person because of some expertise they have, that expertise is only going to be effective if tapped into with an organized conversation. Before you call you need to know how the discussion will solve whatever issue is at stake. Furthermore, the other person will best be able to contribute if they know what map you're working with. Let them know where the conversation is expected to go and how you intend to get there. Maybe, after first identifying the central issue, you'll want to offer some background that will provide the necessary context to the conversation. Then you might present the new data. And, finally, ask for their opinion on how this new data can be applied to the issue at hand, in light of that context. This is a map to the conversation.

4. *Speak slower than you think is necessary.* It's kind of surprising that we can all understand each other when we speak. There are no spaces between sentences or even words. Hardly even any punctuation. Yet, amazingly, somehow we can all understand each other. However, urgency or nervousness can increase our speech rate to such a degree that it begins to hinder comprehension. Even if you're certain you're not speaking too fast, it's always better to err on the side of caution. Speaking more slowly always sounds more professional, reflective and intelligent. And, of course, it increases the ease of comprehension for the listener. Always make an effort to speak more slowly than you think is necessary.

5. *Do not interrupt.* Interruptions are annoying and inefficient. You called this person for their input into the solution to your problem. Let them gather their thoughts and provide you the benefit of a fully formulated answer or explanation. Also, try to avoid putting them in a position interrupt you: always complete your thought with a verbal fade out, so they know when you've finished that point and it's appropriate for them to respond. We usually do this naturally, but it's a good idea to consciously check in and be sure you're following this practice. Avoiding interruptions, on both sides, allows for a more courteous and productive discussion.

6. *Be dressed.* I'm serious. A lot of consultants do a lot of work from home. It's so tempting to take a casual approach to your attire at home. This is a mistake, especially when making phone calls. Your attire affects your disposition. You almost can't help taking on a more laid-back demeanor when you're dressed in a tank top, shorts and sandals. Don't think

5 - Communication Skills Mastery

that just because the other person can't see you, they won't pick up on your tone of unprofessionalism. If you dress for business, you'll feel prepared for business, which will make you sound ready for business. Wear a crisp shirt, dress pants and shoes, at least. You would be surprised what your client can "see" in what they hear.

7. *Listen and confirm.* Obviously, the purpose of your phone call will be defeated if you're not attending to what the other person is saying. It is important to go beyond merely hearing what is said, to confirming what you heard. At appropriate intervals, take a moment to repeat what the other person said. You might preface it with a standard line, like: "So what I hear you saying is that ..." Then, restate in your own words. You can even end your restatement with a question, asking them to confirm you've actually understood what they said. This strategy not only assures the other person that you understand what they are saying, but it also confirms for you that you're getting the information you need to solve the problem or address the issue that motivated the call in the first place.

8. *Review and summarize.* Expanding on the intermittent confirmations along the course of your conversation, at the end of the call, review the key points touched upon and any conclusions or decisions that resulted from the call.

9. *Provide email follow-up.* After the review and summary allows the two of you to explicitly agree on the content of your conversation, put it in writing and send a follow-up email. This allows you to confirm one more time that you're both on the same page while also creating a permanent electron-

ic record which you both can refer to in the future should any confusion arise down the road.

These are ten valuable strategies for getting the most out of your phone communication. Get advance agreement that the time is right for the conversation you would like to have. Reconfirm that agreement if the call runs long. Open with a precise statement of what you want to achieve in the conversation and offer a map for how you see the discussion proceeding and how that structure can address the issue at hand. Be concise and crisp and always speak more slowly than you think necessary. Clarity is essential for success. Don't interrupt and don't give the other person reason to interrupt you. Be dressed for the call in a professional manner. Confirm what the other person is saying intermittently in the course of the call, then provide a summary of the key points and choices or decisions that arose out of the conversation as the call comes to an end. Finally, follow up with a written statement of that summary to ensure both parties are on the same page and that you each have a permanent electronic record of the decisions made for future reference.

Communicating Technical Information to Non-Technical People

This section addresses any situation in which a consultant has to address information that is relatively foreign to the client or the other person in the communication. As emphasized in this book repeatedly, it is the job of the consultant to make it easy for the client to understand and act. The top one percent of consultants are distinguished by their skill to effectively communicate complex information in a way that those untrained in the relevant discipline can comprehend. This ability instills confidence in the client, informs them, and makes it easier for them to make the best decision. All of this, of course, is essential for consultants to fulfill their mission of adding value to their clients' lives and businesses.

Conveying technical information, in an easy to understand way, is of obvious importance and value to consultants. Yet, this is a challenge with which I've seen so many consultants struggle. Why? A big part of the problem is that consultants tend to be very smart in their specialty. Whether it's IT, marketing or organizational culture, they know all the ins and outs and speak all the right jargon. Sometimes the expertise itself becomes a hindrance. For instance, if you're used to explaining issues to those who share your specialty, that comfort may become an obstacle when you find you actually lack the more vernacular language necessary to explain the same issues to someone who doesn't share the common language of your fellow experts.

Let's look at some specific and high-level best practices that are employed by legendary consultants to deal with these kinds of challenges.

1. *Use examples and benchmarks.* For example, you may have to present a set of data to a group of hospital staff indicating that "15 percent of our customers are unsatisfied." Anyone who usually works in customer service, especially those who do statistical analysis in the field, will immediately have a sense of what that means in terms of institutional effectiveness. However, someone in that group with a clin-

ical background, like a physician or nurse, may have no idea what such a figure implies.

i. In that case, it would be beneficial to provide some kind of a *benchmark*. If you followed that customer satisfaction finding with the context that "The number was 10 percent better than the national average," now, the physician or nurse could understand what that statistical finding meant about the hospital's success with customer satisfaction.

ii. You can even improve on that clarification, by providing an *example* that translates these statistics into something more widely accessible. You could explain that "Of the 140 patients we serve every day, 21 leave feeling dissatisfied." It is much easier with these numbers to actually visualize the frequency of dissatisfaction among customers on a daily basis.

iii. Another such approach is what's called *the rule of 10*. This simply involves showcasing complex technical information using the number 10 as the benchmark. This may not be applicable or effective in every scenario but from my experience, it works quite often. People are able to picture 10 of something more easily than fractions or percentages. For example, if we wanted to showcase the buying behaviour of all the customers that walk into a retail store, you might go about it like this: "On average, out of every 10 customers that walk into your store on any given day, 1 customer buys only groceries, 2 customers buy only apparel, 2 buy only electronics, 2 buy only cosmetics, and 3 walk out

5 - Communication Skills Mastery

without a purchase." This description makes it easier for people to picture what is going on and what actions need to be taken to improve a certain aspect of the performance.

iv. *Metaphors* are also useful for making abstract ideas more accessible. Using a metaphor is employing a figure of speech based on its resemblance to the original idea. The idea behind metaphors is that our audience can understand and visualize the comparable metaphor better than our original idea. Metaphors also help us capture attention by making the content more visual and emotionally engaging. For example, if you are a business strategy consultant helping a client design their business improvement plan and wanted to communicate that all components of their business must work together to move the business forward, you might say this: "A business is like a car - it is impossible for it to move forward on an ongoing basis until all different parts and systems work together in alignment." As you can imagine, this statement is much more effective than saying: "For success, all components of your business need to work together in alignment", because the client is able to make a visual connection with the car moving forward. This is powerful.

2. *Don't overkill*. Only present the information that is necessary for the next step. You may be excited about the richer data set and what it bodes for the long-term impact. But you'll only make optimal outcomes more difficult to achieve, if you clutter the steps with unnecessary, futile data. There

may also be the temptation to showcase your work, demonstrate your abilities, to assure them they hired the right person for the job. But in fact, you won't be doing them or yourself any favors if you clutter up the process with self-flattering presentations. The best way you can prove your value to clients is to help them get the results they need. That requires judicious use of research. Additional information, which isn't essential for the purpose at hand, can be presented in a written appendix.

3. *Be prepared for every "so what?"* For every research or data analysis you provide, anticipate your answer if someone asks "so what?" For those without the technical knowledge necessary to make sense of what you're saying, asking "so what" is a perfectly reasonable question. If they don't perceive its importance or relevance, providing that context is your job. If you report that "The business has a 28 percent customer churn rate," what are you going to say when someone asks, "Okay, but so what?" Well, how about something like this, "Of the company's 970 customers it has today, by the end of the year, 272 will have left." That should illustrate what's important about this finding. Again, we can emphasize the relevance of the findings with a benchmark. For example, "This is twice the industry average." For every piece of information you provide, be ready to elaborate on how knowing this information can help the client's business maximize its potential. How does knowing this get the business closer to its goals? Be ready to provide that context. And, going back to the second point, above. If you discover that you can't provide a compelling

"so what" answer, you've maybe discovered a bit of overkill that needs to be cut out of your presentation.

4. *Concluding summary.* As always, we want to summarize. What was presented? What is its relevance? What are the outcomes? Were any decisions made? What are the next steps?

If you'll excuse the pun, communicating technical information to non-technical people is not rocket science. With a few key best practices, you will be able to make effective technical presentations to those who lack your expertise. Remember to support the information with examples and benchmarks. Don't indulge in overkill, make sure everything that's in the presentation is there for a purpose, appropriate for the state of the project at hand. Anticipate the questions that non-technical people are likely to have, so when they ask you "so what," you're ready with techniques, like benchmarks, examples, metaphors, etc. that place the information in a light they'll comprehend and appreciate. And, as always, provide a concluding summary to reinforce what was learned over the course of the presentation, how it's relevant to the business and project, and what next steps are called for as a result.

If all this sounds to you like a bit of preparation overkill of its own, remember: your success depends on the client's success, and the client's success depends on making the very best decision from the best information provided. If you want to consult like the top one percent, you'll need to do the work and have the preparation that allows the top one percent to be legendary consultants. This brings us to the end of the chapter on communications mastery.

This chapter has communicated to you how important communication skills are for successful consulting. Everything else revolves around your ability to be an effective and successful communicator. As one of my mentors observed: you can get away with weaker technical skills if your communication skills are strong. It won't work the other way around though.

Take the time to work on your communication skills. This has been the longest chapter in the book for a good reason. Its importance to the legendary consulting system is immense, and the investment required from you is considerable. Excellent communication skills though, are achievable if you're prepared to put in conscious effort and consistent practice, that will open the door to excellence. I've provided in this chapter a wide range of tips, strategies and best practices that will guide you along the path to raising your communication skills up to the place where you too can be a legendary consultant. I invite you to take this opportunity to transfer your own consulting practice into that top one percent.

« Chapter Six »

Leadership Mastery

"An army of sheep led by a lion can defeat an army of lions led by a sheep."

- African Proverb

A big part of successful consultancy involves the ability to hold the client's hand and lead them across the metaphorical finish line. The term leadership has accumulated a lot of baggage in recent years, as it has been subjected to a wide range of different interpretations. In the consulting context, leadership refers to the practices and conditions that contribute to clients experiencing the consulting process in such a way that leaves them feeling clear, confident, secure and engaged. Good leadership will have the client fully bought into the solutions that the consultant provides. Remember, as I've emphasized previously, in business, the best outcomes usually have less to do with the strategy and more with the implementation.

Ideas, often the right ones, are always floating around. Think in terms of our own life. We know that we need to eat well, exercise, rise early and make the most judicious use of our day, but often we miss out these ideas. A surprising amount of time, the solutions to life's problems are readily available, like low hanging fruit on a tree. Certainly, I'm not saying the strategy is never important, nor that in some circumstances a solid strategy can't be the difference-maker in achieving success. It can provide a competitive advantage. However, most of the time, when you look at the highest performing companies and individuals, it turns out to be effective implementation propelled by powerful leadership that really makes the difference.

That's why our leadership is critical. After all, it isn't usually going to be us, the consultants, implementing the plan, but the client and their team. It is your role to lead that implementation to its greatest success. It is usually through this kind of leadership that you're bringing your value to the clients. It is this leadership that brings their buy-in; it's through this buy-in that commitment and confidence ensure optimum results from your consultancy work.

In earlier chapters, we've emphasized the importance of being your client's trusted advisor. Providing the leadership necessary for success is another important dimension of this role as of trusted advisor. However, in the process of providing such leadership, it is not uncommon to face resistance. The answer to such resistance, as it turns out, is, in fact, effective leadership. Let's be clear though. Such leadership is not about pressuring the clients nor berating the team. If you're leading well, they'll follow, naturally. It is your knowledge, confidence, and enthusiasm that will make the difference. That's what will bring them along.

It is perfectly reasonable for clients or their staff to have concerns and even initial objections. They've been dealing with their company a lot longer than you have. These initial responses can be valuable input for you, but they can also calcify into expressions of resistance: sometimes even less than entirely rational resistance. However, if you've done your homework, if you're prepared, if you've refined your communication and presentation skills, as described earlier in this book, you'll be effectively positioned to lead them beyond these initial doubts and anxieties, toward the brighter future of the change vision. Sometimes this does require taking the bull by the horns; showing them truths they don't see – and perhaps would rather not see.

It's not uncommon for people to be reluctant to acknowledge the shortcomings and possibly even the failures in enterprises in which they have invested a great deal of their time and effort. Furthermore, clients can come from a wide variety of different backgrounds, not all of which equally equip them to recognize when their business may be underperforming or even going off the rails. In these cases, the greatest expression of leadership can simply be allowing them to see the situation through your eyes – the outsider's perspective. At no time though, can you lose sight of the fact that you and the client ultimately have the same goal: making the business thrive; adding value to the client's life. Therefore, it's so important that through the difficulties of such obstacles, you don't allow your thought process to be one of an adversary, but remain that of the leader. It is your job to get the client safely to where they need to be to prosper in business and life.

A big part of achieving that goal is ensuring you have the client's fullest input into the consulting process. Leadership is not about being overbearing. On the contrary, the most effective leadership provides the safety to risk raising any idea which could prove valuable. This includes expressing anxieties about the process, the vision or the strategy. Your leadership facilitates and enables such communication; it does not suppress it.

Prerequisites to Effective Leadership

Let's get our conversation started with consideration of some of the prerequisites to effective consulting leadership. The foremost prerequisite is what I call ego management.

1. *Ego Management.* Ego management should be strong. That is essential for adding value to the client's business. This is especially important when you run into resistance. I've seen some extremely experienced and competent consultants run into problems when they get this wrong. The main downfall here is allowing your ego to cloud the situation when the client does not agree with your opinion. Listening and understanding is a big part of leadership, and if your ego and biases make it difficult to listen and understand openly and attentively to the client's concerns, a major obstacle has risen in your ability to serve as the client's trusted advisor. Ego management is especially valuable to consider once you recognize the importance of the consultant remaining open to learning from the client.

2. *Empathy.* This prerequisite is about being open, receptive and sensitive to the client's position or point of view. Clients may have different kinds of insecurities, fears or concerns. These could be a result of past business – or even personal – experience. Your job as a consultant is to be aware of this potential and to the best of your ability take it into consideration, ensuring that the client feels heard and understood.

3. *Attitude.* Always keep a positive attitude. There's no doubt that in the course of your business with the client things can

become pretty intense and stressful. There are many financial, technical, professional and emotional issues that can come into play, as we have discussed throughout this book. Some periods of tension in working through all this must be expected. Through it all though, the very best attitude you can take is to remain positive. Focus, for instance, on what is working, rather than dwelling on what is not. Pointing your attitude in this direction is how you'll best find your way to the solutions you're seeking.

4. *Evidence over opinion.* Legendary consulting relies on evidence. That is why we never want to be presenting our opinion. Don't focus on intuition; focus on evidence and data. The psychology literature reveals we're all prone to all kinds of failures in our thought processes: confirmation bias, motivated reasoning, and logical fallacies are abundant (Haidt, 2012; Kahan, 2013; Kahan et al., 2012; Kahneman, 2013; Tversky & Kahneman, 1974). The best way to avoid these built-in pitfalls to reasoning is to be sure you're always basing yourself on the evidence: the hard data. Failing to do this will only ensure that your client and others will push back against your work and analysis. And why shouldn't they? Their opinion is just as good as yours! Unless of course, you have the evidence to back up what you're saying. Leave your opinion parked in the garage, drive into the future on the wheels of the actual evidence that informs your arguments. And, let's not kid ourselves, we're all prone to deceiving ourselves (Alexander, 1982; Smith, 2007; Trivers, 2014). The best way for you to be most confident about your ideas and recommendations is to know you've

grounded them in the empirical data right from the start.

5. *Invitations over assertions.* This is a subtle tweak of your leadership approach. It particularly concerns your ability to bring the client along in the process. It has been implicit in the very definition of leadership we've been using. Strong leadership does not come from overpowering or overwhelming the client; we aren't trying to bludgeon them into submission. The success of the legendary consulting system depends on the client's full buy-in, and that can only come from a voluntary commitment to join the enterprise. Don't insist the client subscribe to your beliefs, arguments, ideas, analyses or visions. Instead, offer an invitation, which is as enticing as you can make it. The invitation will be accepted if you've done your homework. It's here where your aggressive persistence needs to be directed, doing your homework, not in badgering the client to accept your vision. Many good consultants have fallen short of legendary achievement because they've failed to appreciate the importance of this distinction: always, offer invitations, do not push assertions.

These are the prerequisites to successful leadership: manage your ego; empathize with your clients' concerns, expressed and unexpressed; maintain a positive attitude; always emphasize evidence over opinion; when facing resistance; and do not push assertions, but offer the most enticing, best informed invitations to join you in your analyses, conclusions and vision. These are the basic approaches that provide the foundation for effective leadership as a consultant.

Key Practices and Strategies for Effective Leadership

It is true that leadership is an art that will be enhanced with practice and experience. However, not all practice and experience are created equal. You can jump the learning curve by focusing your efforts in appropriate ways. Your guide for this focus comes from the beacon provided by the practices of the best leaders in the consulting world – the top one percent. Let me share with you some of these key practices.

1. *Walk them through the process.* We have discussed the importance of this in building relationships and positioning, so I will keep this brief. Great consultants, once they enter into a new consulting arrangement, carefully walk their clients, step by step, through the processes they'll be experiencing. This practice creates an open dialogue. The process becomes transparent, enabling the client to feel secure, engaged and enthused.

2. *Appreciate and elevate.* This is a key practice which I've come to identify. Consulting is about bringing people on board. It's the lifeblood of the enterprise. We need clients to buy-in, stakeholders to join the team. I've noticed over my years of consulting that it is those consultants who recognize and acknowledge the skills, abilities, attitudes, and achievements of others – particularly their clients and the clients' teams – who are most able to attract others to enthusiastically join their vision and help them achieve their goals. They magnetically attract people and their support. Once attracted, the consultant can elevate these people to

the next level. This is how a legendary consultant generates value for the client: elevating everyone's performance to a higher level. I invite you to make this a core practice in your consulting work, irrespective of the number of clients you are working with: always strive to appreciate others and what they offer. Furthermore, express that appreciation; don't be stingy with praise. And, make that praise concrete and tangible. Even small approbations can go a long way in encouraging others and inspiring their commitment to the project. It's through that commitment that you can elevate them, improving their work and even their life, while adding value to their business.

3. *Present recommendations carefully.* When you're trying to lead your client toward the best solution for the business, you want to follow the lead of the legendary consultants: always provide your recommendations with the appropriate structure and level of detail. Remember, presenting a recommendation successfully, is similar to closing a sale. People will be reluctant to buy if they feel insufficiently informed, but information overload can also go against a sale, as the potential buyer may simply back away defensively. Too little or too much information can get in the way of a sale. You need to have evidence to support your position, but you also need to be cognizant of details. An avalanche of data won't persuade a prudent buyer. Always treat your client as though that's exactly who they are. The recommendation phase is critical to success. You do need to come to the meeting armed to the teeth with the data and work findings that inform your recommendations. How much of

that data you actually use, depends on your careful assessment of what the client knows, needs to know, even wants to know. Exerting the appropriate level of informed care in the recommendation process can be the most powerful practice of all.

4. *Often ask for feedback and suggestions.* As we've discussed, not all clients are comfortable voicing an opinion, especially when dealing with someone they've brought in as an expert. Yet, your job is to add value to the client's life and business. How can you do that if the client isn't optimally forthcoming? Here, the responsibility falls on you as the consultant. You have to regularly solicit the client's feedback, ask them for suggestions on how to tackle specific challenges in the consulting process. Again, this sounds obvious, but you would be surprised how many consultants get caught up in their own vision and fail to sufficiently check in with clients to ensure they're actually onboard with the process. Without the client onboard, you don't have their buy-in, and you're certainly not regarded as the trusted advisor. So, make a point to regularly check in on the client's suggestions or other feedback throughout the process.

5. *Lead change strategically.* Most consulting involves some kind of change or planning for change in the client's business. When that's what you're doing, it is critical to be strategic (Kotter, 2002). Handle the change, and its impacts, strategically. Humans are creatures of habit; most of us grow uncomfortable with change – even when we know it's for the better. As evolved organisms, we primarily want to survive and if the status quo brought us this far, messing with

it seems counterintuitive. That's why you always come to the consulting engagement armed with the empirical data that points to the benefits of change and the direction necessary to achieve those benefits. Keep in mind rational decision making, and emotional thought are not the same thing. Even when people know a coming change is beneficial, denial is often the reflexive response. People will reject it consciously and even more often subconsciously. This is why change leadership needs to be strategic. A good rule of thumb in this regard is to follow the change formula created by David Gleicher back in the 1960s (Gleicher, 1961). Start by strategically triggering dissatisfaction with the status quo. However logical the preferred condition of an imagined new future is, people will feel far more motivated to pursue that future if they are less comfortable with their present state. Shift the strategic focus from selling the future to unmasking the ills of the present. Only when people see the present isn't as comfy as they thought it was, will they be genuinely motivated to make the changes required to enter that new future.

6. *Generate quick wins.* This is another valuable strategic practice. It aligns with Kotter's eight-step change model (Kotter, 2002). One of his steps is, precisely, generating quick wins. The strategic value in such a practice is demonstrating to the client, and everyone involved, that beneficial change is possible, regardless of how entrenched the former deficiencies may have seemed. Quick wins are inspirational and illustrative. Far too often changes in business, or life, in fact, do not provide tangible results and identifiable bene-

fits. Given the denial about change mentioned above, such an experience with ineffectual change will understandably create in most of us reservation and even skepticism about the prospect of change. Generating quick wins dispels that skepticism, motivates buy-in and inspires enthusiasm. No one wants to expend energy just to waste their time. The quick win shows everyone that their energy is well spent. It's an investment in a better future condition.

7. *Be aware of the transition.* No one gets from a present state to a future one without passing through a transition of some sort. Think of it this way: change is not an event; it's a process! Conscious awareness of the fact that companies and individuals need time to accept, accommodate and implement change makes us more effective change leaders. This leads us directly to the next key practice in leadership mastery.

8. *Set the right expectations.* Being realistic is essential for establishing the rapport you need to be successful; win others on your team; and position yourself as the client's trusted advisor. Think of this in terms of the project's scope. Often a consulting project completely loses its direction. The scope shifts, is sidetracked or diluted. When this happens, the initial objectives of the project remain unrealized. The client does not see the promised value added. This frankly is a failure. Success, therefore, requires the consultant, right from the start, to be clear about the expectations: what is and is not the scope of the project? What are the timelines? What outcomes can be expected? If these expectations are clearly identified from the start, when you deliver them,

the client comes away from the experience satisfied that you did as you promised and their business is better off for having worked with you. Indeed, within reasonable limits, I would urge you to under promise. If you under promise, you can over deliver. Think of it this way, if you promise 1x, and deliver 2x, the reward is 3x. Set the right expectations.

9. *When hurried, take your time.* As mentioned earlier, consulting projects can get intense. You're in difficult dialogue with clients, facilitating sessions, trying to convey ideas, get others onboard, etc. It's at these times that the sudden appearance of resistance may be most off-putting. Perhaps amid all this, an email pops into your inbox, which challenges some aspect of the process. You're feeling hurried, with so much on the go, there's a great temptation to dive right in there and shoot off a rapid response; you didn't even want to see this, you certainly don't want it lingering in the to-do pile. That though, is when you most need to take your time. When you feel most pressured to respond, that is exactly when you are most likely to misjudge the correct response. That's when mistakes are most common. And the first mistake would be rushing a reply. The pressure-packed clock ticking in your head isn't the real movement of time. You have time to sit back and consider. It might be tactically wise to shoot off a quick recognition: perhaps a couple of lines to the effect, "let me think about that" or "I'll have to gather information to reply." If you feel you need to buy yourself that time, that's fine. But above all, be sure to give yourself the time you need to avoid the kind of mistakes that so often result from hurried replies. Fast is good, but right is better. Vitally

important to effective leadership is doing all you can to get it right.

These are key, important practices for providing the most powerful consulting leadership. They're the practices that distinguish the legendary consultants from the rest. Walk clients through the process, quantifying and defining the steps, so they know what's coming and are ready for it. Appreciate people's accomplishments and abilities. Praise them for their achievements and leverage that appreciation to help elevate them to a higher level, where more value can be created in their lives and business. Make sure your recommendations are well informed, but not overloaded. Present your recommendations carefully, aware of the audience and the situation. Not everyone is equally as comfortable with expressing their concerns or suggestions, especially when dealing with an expert hired precisely to implement change based on their expertise. To ensure the highest level of buy-in and support be sure to regularly solicit feedback and suggestions. Be strategic about the changes you lead. Cultivate a dissatisfaction with the present, so people are more motivated to facilitate the changes that will lead them into a new future. Generate quick wins, so everyone recognizes that beneficial change is possible and happening. Be aware that all change is a process, that way you can enable the transition to a positive experience. Set the right expectations. It's better to under promise so that you can over deliver. When hurried, take your time. Don't allow the pressure of the situation to cause you to make the pressure worse through an unnecessary mistake. Take the time you need to get it right.

Handling Client Objections

A central challenge in consulting is keeping everybody onboard. You want to ensure that you have the client and the client's entire team traveling alongside as you move forward with your project. It is inevitable though, however much all parties agree on the desired value-increasing outcome, differences of opinions will arise. From vision to strategy to tactics, there will be a variety of areas in which objections will arise. Now, obviously, there's no magic pill to remedy this; no one-size-fits-all solutions can be prepared to answer all these objections in advance. However, in my experience, there are four key approaches that can get you close to having all your bases covered.

1. *Ask questions, rather than give answers.* This is, of course, a reiteration of one of the key practices in leadership mastery, discussed above. It's so important though, it deserves reiteration. When someone objects to ideas, instead of trying to answer their objection and trying to convince them of the virtues of your approach, often it is much more effective to ask them a question and actively listen to their answer. There are a few benefits to this approach.

    i. This is an opportunity to get better clarity on the objection. What exactly is the source of the disagreement? The person making the objection may have thought of something you had not. Before you start telling them why you're right, it would be wise to be sure you understand what they are saying as deeply as you reasonably can.

ii. Also, this approach helps the client better understand the deeper foundations of their objection. Perhaps they had really tapped into something important, but it's also possible the objection is the result of an assumption based on nothing more than a bias for the familiar or the expression of anxiety about change. Interrogating the objection can help clarify these kinds of issues.

iii. Finally, this approach buys you a little time to collect your thoughts and better determine the nature of the reply you'll provide. Is this an objection best answered with an appeal to raw data or is this one that requires emotional awareness and metaphorical handholding to help the client get over the fears?

Some questions you can ask might be: "Can you tell me more about that?"; "Can you elaborate on that?"; "Why is that important?"; "What makes you feel that way?"; "Is there evidence to support this?"; or "Has this worked in the past?" All of these questions push the client, or person making the objection, to dig deeper into an understanding of the underlying foundations of their beliefs. Objections often arise as reflexes; these types of questions probe the mechanisms giving rise to the reflex. They help you get to the real crux of the objection.

Another question, which I often use in my practice, which can be an alternative or supplement to those listed above is: "Are you willing to hear my perspective?" When the objection is not driven by evidence or logic, but rather psychological responses, inviting the person making the objection to open themselves to another perspective can be a valuable and effective form of bridge building, from their state of anxiety to one of greater openness to new possibilities.

The next three approaches discussed are along the lines of frameworks you can use to present your positions. The Socratic Method only gets us so far; at some point, we have to make a case for our recommendations.

2. *Feel, Felt, Found.* This approach was taught to me by one of my mentors. It's a powerful response to objections. Each term serves as a touchstone along the path of a statement of empathy and resolution. That statement put concisely, is this: I know how you feel; I have felt the same way; let me tell you what I've found. This is similar in technique to the bridge building question, "Are you willing to hear my perspective?" But it is even more powerful because it places you in sympathetic alliance with the person making the objection, right from the start. A rapport is established which not only allows but is actually premised upon, the smooth movement from the state of objection to the state of resolution.

   I have used this approach hundreds of times and can report that it works wonders. Now, obviously, this kind of thing opens the possibility for emotional manipulation. I urge you to restrict your use of this powerful tool to only those situations in which you honestly have felt the same way as the objector. Such restriction is not only more ethical, but it makes the approach more powerful, as your natural empathy will be observed by the person making the objection.

3. *Lessons learned.* This is another game changer. Every time I use it, it completely transforms the client's, or other ob-

jector's, approach to the situation. This works as a plug-and-play template. The idea is that you go through the approaches discussed above, asking questions, empathizing, and so on. But when the time comes to present your own ideas, this is what you say: "I understand where you're coming from, but based on my experience of working on similar projects, in the past, let me share with you what I have learned." From there, you go on to explain the experience behind the reasons for your recommendation.

Again, this approach opens with empathy for where the objector is, right now. In a smooth transition, then, as a kind of proxy for the objector, you then move to what experience has taught you, despite your appreciation of the objection. It invites the objector to be open to learning by proxy the same lesson from experience that you had to learn the hard way. And, of course, there is a certain authority in the experiences you've had. None of those present likely were there. Here, you take the high ground as the voice of experience from the school of hard knocks. They would be wise to heed the warnings of this scout from their own possible future fiascos.

4. *Understand and invite.* In this approach, you again start off from a place of empathy, before moving on to possible answers to the objection. "I understand what you're thinking, here's what I would invite you to consider." This is a little more abrupt transition from empathy to solution than the options discussed above. You might use it if you don't sense the objection is so emotionally wrought. It still uses a soft landing method to get to the solution. You're not insisting,

arguing, or defending; you're simply inviting the objector to consider something further. I think of "invite" as a magical word. There's a generosity and courtesy to it. It asks the other person to share an insight or experience with you: to make common cause in the pursuit of truth and wisdom.

These are the four approaches I recommend you master for fielding objections. First is to ask questions, to better understand the objection and the reasons or feelings behind it. The *Feel, Felt, Found* framework allows us to gradually move an objector from a state of mutual appreciation to the insights of experience. Both the *Lessons Learned* and *Understand and Invite* frameworks have similar dynamics. In all these cases, we're trying to move the objector from a current state of anxiety to one informed by experience. They differ primarily in the degree of delicacy involved in helping the objector make that transition. In all cases, we need to start by standing with the objector, taking their objection seriously, then using that empathy and rapport, and its related feelings of trust, to help the objector come to appreciate what experience has taught us about similar of situations in the past.

This brings us to the final dimension of leadership mastery.

Leadership with Difficult People

Dealing with difficult people is where leadership gets challenging. People bring a rich palette of different backgrounds, experiences, knowledge, attitudes, and biases to the table in any collaborative project. Certainly, in some situations, such as finding outside-the-box solutions, this diversity can be beneficial.

However, like everything, there are trade-offs, and this diversity of personality is no different. To be clear, I'm not talking about bad people or people with malevolent intentions. It's just a fact of life that sometimes, some personalities don't mesh well in a collaborative context.

Business, in general, involves so much of human life, the terrain for spurring conflict between personal differences is easily breached. From the chilly cold shoulder to outright arguments, counterproductive consequences can appear in many forms. Then you add in dispositional considerations, like the fact that some people are less conscientious than others and don't always meet their deadlines. Some people, due to a range of past experiences, including real or perceived offenses, are inclined to be short-tempered or ill-mannered with other specific individuals – or even other people in general. Working with groups of people can be a proverbial minefield. Yet, working with others is exactly what consulting is all about. The legendary consulting system enables you to provide the leadership that gets your clients and your teams through those minefields, safely and productively.

How do you deal with difficult people like only the top one percent can? To start, this is another of those situations in which there's no magic pill. People are different in a host of ways. What works for one is never guaranteed to work for another. Still, there are some best practices that I'm sure will increase your likeliness of success in dealing with difficult people. Let's have a look:

1. *Examine yourself.* When there's a friction between you and another person, start by examining yourself. What are you contributing to that friction? Have you in fact been per-

forming at your best? As professional as you can be? Responding to their correspondence appropriately and in a timely manner? Maybe there's something you're doing which is triggering the response from the other person that you're finding so difficult. My mother used to say, it takes two hands to clap. You're one of those hands in this relationship. What can you do to change the dynamic on your end? That's the most straightforward solutions of all, isn't it?

2. *Approach the situation with a clear goal.* We've all been in situations where a conflict has been left to fester and subsequently led to all kinds of further difficulties that continue to have people run around putting out fires. Far more efficient than trying to keep on top of every small localized manifestation is to return to the source of the difficulty and resolve it. If you're going to avoid this constant sidetracking of your agenda with localized side fires, clarity is going to provide the power you need to cut to the root of the problem. Identify what is it precisely that you need from that relationship? What does it have to accomplish for your consulting project to succeed? Do you want an approval, a referral, access, a submission or a part of a deliverable? First, identify what's needed. You can only resolve the core difficulty if you're clear about the direction you need it to be resolved.

3. *Talk in person.* Group dynamics affect relationships. Fear of losing face is a powerful motivator for people to entrench their position and apply their imagination, not to solutions, but reasons why they're right. In psychology, they call it motivated reasoning. As the research of Dan Kahan of Yale University and his colleagues has shown, every-

one is subject to motivated reasoning, however smart or educated they are (Kahan, 2013; Kahan et al., 2012). And, motivated reasoning is most powerfully activated in a public setting. A far more likely approach to get past such dynamics is to talk to the person in a one-on-one setting. Fear and ego won't be entirely eliminated in an in-person talk, but it will be significantly reduced. As such, it provides us more opportunity for working around it, to get at diplomatically reasoned solutions.

4. *Don't take it personally.* When you're grappling with a difficult person or situation, that's preventing you from achieving the excellence toward which you're striving, it's so easy to take it personally. Why is this person undermining me? The truth is, in such contexts, there are always so many things going on. Most of which either are out of your sight or predate your arrival. The fact that you're dealing with the fallout doesn't mean it's about you or even directed at you. Chances are, you're just in the wrong place and time given some other bit of history. Once you remove your own ego and hurt feelings from the equation, it becomes much easier to just think of this as another business problem that needs to be worked out to move the project forward.

5. *Listen.* Listening has come up time and again in this book because it is the most powerful weapon we have in dealing with people and situations of all kinds. Always be sure that you're listening. Nothing perpetuates a conflict more than being unwilling or unable to listen. I've seen so many apparently intractable situations almost magically resolved just by an overt willingness to listen. Sit with people, ask them

questions, and better understand what their concerns are. You can't solve their problem if you don't understand them. And, sometimes it's as simple as someone just needing to feel that they have been heard. Often, people don't even realize that they're being difficult just to get attention, just to feel they're not insignificant. Moralizing over such things does you no good. You have a job to do. Sit down with the person; allow them to be sincerely heard. It will move your project forward and might even make a friend out of a former adversary.

6. *Meet them where they are.* In the discussion above on leadership approaches, we emphasized the importance of connection. To create a connection you want to ensure that you do not make them defensive, instead meet them where they are. This means showcasing empathy and presenting yourself as someone similar to them. Once you have met them where they are, you can slowly inspire them to change and move toward the solution.

These best practices are all great tools for leading difficult people. Indeed, throughout this book, I've provided you a wide range of interpersonal and relationship tools and strategies that can be used to deal with all variety of social complications that arise at the workplace and in the consulting environment in particular. I'm confident, if you can absorb the lessons taught here, there's no such workplace conflict that you won't be able to gracefully handle.

However, if none of these social negotiation tools and strategies work, let me leave you with two more examples of best practices to which you can always turn.

1. *Limit their access to you.* If you've tried everything discussed above, in this chapter and this book, and still the conflict persists, simply limit that person's access to you. Put yourself out of their reach. If the difficult person is anyone other than your core client, this can be done easily. Do not respond to their emails unless you really need to. Avoid one-on-one meeting with them. Try to bypass them on your route to client's success as much as possible.

2. *Build support around you.* If all your efforts to resolve the problem prove futile, you need to concentrate on building your support. You need to build coalitions around your ideas, your recommendations and especially your vision. The best way to build these coalitions is in offline, one-on-one relationships. Identify those who can be instrumental in getting each stage in your project implemented and make a concerted effort to win their support. Gradually, one person at a time, you can erect a walk that shelters the project from that difficult person that threatened to undermine your efforts.

Remember, at the end of the day, what all this is about is your ability to add value to the client's business. If someone is so difficult and impervious to all your bridge mending appeals, that the project is endangered, it is your responsibility to do whatever it takes to enable you to effectively deliver those valuable solutions for which you were hired.

In summary, when your leadership is confronted with difficult people, start by examining yourself. Are you contributing to the problem and if so how? What can you do about it? When assessing the situation, remain clear about your goal. How does this difficult person fit into the larger picture? What is it you need from them to achieve your goal? Talk to the difficult person in a private context. Get away from the complications and distractions of a group setting so you might be able to minimize fears and ego and work out solutions together. However things go, don't take it personally. Even if it really were personal, getting offended and indignant will solve nothing. You're always entering a client world that has its own history and dynamics. At most you're likely a convenient target. Listen carefully and sincerely to what the difficult person has to say. Perhaps you haven't adequately understood their objection. Or maybe the person simply needs to be heard for their own personal reasons. Try to meet them where they and inspire them to change. However, if none of this works, after all your best and most earnest efforts, it may just be necessary to cut the difficult person out of the loop. Reduce their access to you and build around yourself an alliance of support that will allow you to get the project done.

This brings us to the end of our discussion of the prerequisites, approaches and best practices for leadership mastery in the consulting business.

« CHAPTER SEVEN »
Quality Mastery

"Quality is never an accident. It is always the result of intelligent effort."

- JOHN RUSKIN

We now come to the last mastery area in the legendary consulting system. Consultants are often employed because of their ability to deliver high-quality work to their client. The delivery of quality is a major consideration not only in relation to the value a consultant provides to their clients but in terms of the consultant's ability to generate repeat business. Quality is at the heart of the entire consulting profession. Therefore we consultants must put quality at the center of our attention and practice. Whether we're talking about writing a letter, delivering a presentation, or providing a set of recommendations, it is incumbent upon us to conduct our business in a way that produces the highest possible quality.

To achieve that end, it is important to always keep in mind that, contrary to how some might perceive it, quality is not an event or an act, it is a process. More than that, it is a result, a product of a correct process. You achieve quality when you're doing things right. The legendary consultants, those who consistently provide high-quality service to their clients, are the ones who get these important things right, consistently. What are these things and how do you go about getting them right? These are questions we'll answer in this chapter.

A matter that often comes up regarding quality is whether it's in the eye of the beholder or meets some objective standard. In a certain sense, all quality judgments are matters of perception: even an objective metric is only of value to the degree it is valued by a particular individual. That, of course, doesn't change the fact that despite anyone's perception of a standard, they certainly can, and often do, use objective metrics to measure whether that standard has been met. Consultants aspire to increase the value of their clients' lives and businesses, but the clients will often have very specific, objective metrics and standards for whether that has been accomplished or not.

Talking about quality, then, we are always placed somewhere between these sensibilities of personal perception and the hard metrics that inform such perceptions. Legendary consultants are the ones who understand this fact about quality and effectively tailor their consulting services to meet the quality expectations and standards of their clients. How do they do this? In this chapter, I'll share with you my study on how the top one percent do precisely that. This process of tailoring quality to the client is built around five pillars that underpin it. Let's first have a look at what those are.

Five Pillars of Quality

1. *Reliability.* The more reliable the consultant is, the higher the perception of the quality of the consultant's service.

This reliability is established in the minor details of everyday activity. Meeting deadlines, replying to emails in a timely manner, being on time for meetings, doing as you say, and keeping your word: Conducting your business in a timely and consistent manner gradually cultivates the impression of being reliable.

2. *Impact.* A considerable influence on a client's perception of the quality of your service will be the impact it has on their business. This is the objective side of quality: did you improve revenues or decrease expenses? Whatever you were brought in to do, did you meet the bottom line? Did you deliver? Did you have the impact you were hired to have? As I've emphasized over and over again in this book, the work of the consultant is to add value to the client's life or business. The impact is the consideration of the degree to which you've done so. And the client will experience this impact as the quality of your service.

3. *Responsiveness.* This pillar dovetails with the reliability pillar, but more specifically addresses the role of effective and transparent communication. Highly responsive consultants, in my experience, build a strong feeling of trust and reliability in the mind of their clients. This funnels into a perception of quality for that client. And, take note, responsiveness doesn't necessarily mean having all the answers at the drop of a hat. Sometimes you do need some time, to reflect or research. That's fine. But don't leave the client or team member hanging, while you do so. Getting back to them and letting them know you'll need a little more time, but will get back to them by tomorrow – or whatever window of time

is appropriate – is also practicing high responsiveness. On the part of the person asking a question or raising an issue, some uncertainty is necessarily entailed; they're moving the discussion from one of relative certainty to one of relative uncertainty. There's usually an unease about what's going to come from this shift into lowered certainty. By providing a prompt reply, even if only to say you'll respond the next day, you've restored that feeling of certainty. Yes, the question needs to be answered, but things are moving forward in an orderly manner. You are letting them know you're on top of the situation and are dealing with it. That restored certainty goes a long way in cultivating in their perception the quality of the service you're providing.

It should be mentioned, here, that there is a danger of excessive responsiveness. It is possible to spend all your time responding to other people's anxieties. And indeed excessively responding can even feed the dynamic; if you respond reassuringly to every little worry, the other person is more likely to rely on you as a source of comfort every time they have a little concern. As important as responsiveness is, there has to be a balance with other priorities. The challenge is to find that sweet spot where your responsiveness is constructive and productive for all involved and doesn't veer off in the opposite direction.

4. *Character.* Who are you as a person and how does that contribute to the quality of your consulting work? Being honest, conscientious, ethical, sincere, is critical to creating that trusted advisor status that best serves your client. This stuff is hard to fake. If you're involved in a lengthy project with

a client, they're going to figure out before too long what is the true nature of your character. Cultivating these qualities in yourself, as genuine expressions of who you are, is crucial to legendary consulting. Possessing and expressing such character is at the very heart of the client's perception of the quality of your service. If they do not like you or trust you, their perception of your service can be expected to be severely compromised.

5. *Visual Appearance.* Here the emphasis is placed primarily on the look and feel of your products. Is your project report, your slide deck, proposal, etc., visually well put together: is the formatting effective, is the look consistent, and is your writing grammatically accurate? All of these things have a huge impact on the perception of the quality of your work.

The five pillars that underpin quality in the consulting business, then, are reliability, doing what you say you'll do; impact, actually having measurable positive effects on your client's life or business; responsiveness, getting back to people promptly, so that they feel secure in the belief that you're on top of the situation; character, genuinely being an honest, conscientious, ethical and sincere person; and visual appearance, ensuring that the look and feel of your material products is clear and effective. All of these demonstrates your value to the client, which cultivates in them, a perception of the quality of your service.

Let's take a moment here to recognize that in fact all the mastery areas we've discussed through this book –personal, proposal, relationship and positioning, communication, leadership, etc. – all of these, when effectively performed, build the perception of you as a consultant who provides high-quality services. In a certain sense, this entire book has been about the things you can do to cultivate the client's perception of your work as that of the highest quality. In this chapter, we're focusing on specific strategies particularly aimed at improving the perception of your consulting work's quality.

Let's dive into some of these strategies.

Seven Strategies for Quality Improvement

1. *Planning.* We've already addressed the fact that consultants who practice their craft like the top one percent distinguish themselves in their capacity for robust planning. (You see, by now, how the threads of these common themes continually weave throughout the narrative.) Let's dig a little deeper into this idea. Every project requires time set aside for planning. Nothing legendary is achieved without sufficient planning. Obviously, this isn't an invitation to fall into paralysis by over-analysis: the work has to be done. But, as the old line goes: not planning is planning to fail. Making it up as you go along is not a recipe for success. Let's break this strategy down into some specific techniques.

    i. An important aspect of planning is to set the project up in the planning phase. Block off your schedule, hold your discussions with the client, plan team meetings, establish deadlines, etc., all at the very start of the project. The initial planning stage could last anywhere from three to ten days. There's often research that needs to be conducted during this period so it can be a bit variable. Be sure, during this time, that all the parameters are clear and everyone is onboard with the project and their own responsibilities. Having all this locked in place from the start can be a game changer in terms of delivering high quality outputs and achieving maximum success.

ii. Start at the end. This is a powerful technique for all aspects of business and life. It has in fact been extremely important in the writing of this book. Imagine, right from the start, what your final deliverable will look like. Visualize it. Doing this is a form of hacking your brain chemistry to get the most out of your potential and motivation. Starting at the end, in this way, creates a huge dopamine rush. Dopamine is a neural chemical that generates feelings of pleasure when we accomplish something that's important to us. Think of that feeling you have when you cross off a significant accomplishment on your to-do list. That's dopamine rewarding you for your efforts.

By starting at the end, we are in a sense fooling ourselves into thinking we're closer to the end than we really are. In the process, we're also developing powerful, pleasurable associations with the completion of that project, which motivates us to get it done. Think of how much more pleasurable the dopamine rush will be when we really do finish the project.

How do you go about this, starting from the end? For example, imagine you have a 15-page report that needs to be produced. Start by imagining a title that will convey the important message or lesson to be taken from that report. Use that title to create an aesthetically pleasing cover page. Identify the names or themes of the different components of the report. Sure, you can change them later, but for now, we want to feel the excitement of how it's all going to look when it's done. Now, you have a template, that conjures in your mind what the final project will look like, and you can start to fill in the blanks. That's just what I did when I first laid out the plan for this book. I had the title page and listed nine chapters including introduction and conclusion that covered the topics I considered important. Even before I knew the names of the chapters – and they've changed throughout the writing process, anyway – just knowing how it was to be laid out, having the plan in front of me, allowed me to visualize what the book would look like. The dopamine rush that came with this initial visualization created a huge motivation to push forward the fully fleshed out writing of the book. Whatever you have to do, from writing a book to delivering a slide deck, to composing a report, by starting at the end, your visualization process can hack your dopamine reward center, to inspire you in the realization of your plans.

Planning is a huge game changer. Plan the heck out of your projects. All these techniques discussed above – establishing the project in the planning phase and starting from the end – are all ways you can leverage the most powerful results with the most effective planning strategies. Planning does front-load the work, with the result that sometimes you don't feel like you're making as much progress – however, if you've created the right benchmarks, you'll know when that worry is baseless. But nothing I've observed more clearly distinguishes the average consultant from the legendary consultant than robust and conscientious planning.

2. *Building the right team.* Conscious and deliberate awareness of who is (or is not) included in your team is crucially important to the success of any consulting project. Obviously, there are many variables that come into play, including the size or type of the client's business, the nature of the project, and your own consulting practice. Some of us find ourselves working alone on many of our projects. Unless that's the case, however small or large, you will need to build a team. Understanding how to do that in a way that contributes to the project's success is vital.

   i. A good rule of thumb is to always build a team that supports your strengths by building to compensate for your weaknesses. Hiring someone who has the same strengths as you is redundant. This approach is counter-intuitive though. I have noticed time and again that people are often attracted to people like them, and end up building a team with people having the same strengths as them. Failing to hire someone who compensates for your weaknesses leaves the team underpowered. It creates inefficiencies that will be costly in the long run. Obviously, the first prerequisite to do this is the self-knowledge what your own strengths and weaknesses are - which we analyzed in the personal mastery chapter. An honest inventory, supplemented by the input of others you trust, is an important first step to building the best possible team.

ii. Get a partner from the client's team. When I start a new project, I make sure to ask my client to specifically assign someone to work with me as a partner in leading that engagement. Having such a team mate has tremendous value. This partner provides me a wide range of insights about the nature of the business problem we're addressing, the dynamics of the company or peculiarities of the industry. Having an inside team member has many other benefits too. For instance, it can pave the way for getting timely meeting appointments with key stakeholders. Also, think about if your project involves making changes in the systems or culture of the company; how much easier is that going to be if someone the other stakeholders know and trust is on your side when these changes are being discussed. Having such a partner, when you consider the doors they can open, the off-book organizational knowledge they can provide, can dramatically transform your capacities and effectiveness. When looking for such a partner look for someone who is respected and influential within the organization. Also, experience within the main scope of the project is vitally valuable.

iii. Build a strong relationship with administrative support staff. You know the old joke that it's the secretaries who really run the offices. Establishing a good relationship with support staff can go a long way in advancing the cause of your project. (And, on the other side, don't kid yourself: if you mistreat these people, they often have the means to sabotage your efforts.) You might be the exciting new kid in the office, but if you think you're a big shot and take the administrative support staff for granted, in the end, it's you who'll likely pay the price. If it doesn't break you, buying them coffee and donuts occasionally, or having a nice lunch with them expressing appreciation for their support, can build some serious goodwill. In any case, there's no reason not to always be courteous and respectful in your dealings with them.

3. *Build processes and rituals that support quality.* I am sure you know very well the vital importance of building processes: they make your life far easier. They make your work better, more predictable, and efficient. Let's look at some valuable processes and rituals.

   i. *Weekly reflection meetings.* This is a way to build into your process a regular taking stock. It's a valuable ritual for determining that everyone is onboard and things are progressing consistently with the stakeholders' and clients' understanding and expectation. Someone's genuine misunderstanding can lead things way off the rails if left unaddressed for too long. Weekly reflection meetings, taking stock of how things are going and what's coming next, are important tools for ensuring you're all on the same page. I encourage you to hold such meetings on a weekly basis. Schedule calendar time for these meetings. They're important and deserve to be prioritized.

ii. *Peer reviews.* Before any of your products or outputs are placed in front of your client, they should have been peer reviewed. Show it to those informed enough to assess the product, so that they can provide you constructive criticism on how it might yet be further improved. This is a simple, yet ultra-powerful practice.

iii. *Standardize deliverables.* This is a process that reduces decision making. There is research showing that decision making can be thought of as a muscle. This is something that has been explored extensively in the self-regulation literature (Vohs & Baumeister, 2016). If you overuse your decision-making faculties, you can become fatigued and depleted. Eventually, your overall performance suffers. Streamlining processes, which result in standardized deliverables, alleviates this mental strain. They also benefit you with quality and consistent look for your brand. Create templates for everything you do: Word documents, slideshows, and presentations. Know before you start what fonts, colors, etc., you'll be using, because you've already identified them as your best choice: the brand look that you want to promote. This provides improvements in aesthetics, work time and stress reduction.

iv. *Measure quality.* As discussed above, quality may be mainly perception, what's being perceived can often be quantified, and your ability to do that goes a long way in establishing, objectively, the quality of your services. Furthermore, what is measured is what can and does get addressed. Nebulous premises easily slide by. When we're crunching numbers, we know what has (or hasn't) been accomplished. Admittedly, some outcomes are easier to measure than others. If we set out to increase revenues, the numbers will be there in the bottom line to assess the quality of our intervention. Not all interventions though, so directly lend themselves to bottom-line calculations, for example, improving work culture. That doesn't mean that we can't generate quantifiable results. The obvious approach in such a case is qualitative data use, through application of surveys or focus groups. These can provide concrete data on the effectiveness of the project. A thorough introduction to this topic, especially recommended for the statistically minded, is Lars Lybery and colleagues' great book, *Survey Measurement and Process Quality* (Lyberg et al., 1997). Improvement is the name of the game in consulting. We're often brought in to improve something. But you cannot know if you're succeeding at that unless you have the data to back up your convictions. Quality measurement is essential for both your client's and your own awareness of your achievements.

Build into your consulting work the right processes and rituals. We've discussed several strategies, which I urge you to integrate into your own consulting practice. Establish weekly reflection meetings, to assess progress made and ensure everyone is on the same page moving forward. Conduct peer reviews before any deliverable goes before the client. Use standardized deliverables to reduce your stress, increase your work speed and create a consistent brand for your own business. Finally, always be measuring quality: if you can show it in numbers, the quality speaks for itself.

4. *Engage in deep work*. I learned the value of this strategy through a book by Cal Newport, *Deep Work* (2016). His key insight was that it is challenging to deliver top-drawer work while in a distracted state. I'm sure I don't have to convince you how easy it is to be distracted in today's world. All the social media technology swamps us: texts, tweets, email, phone calls, podcasts, Facebook, and so many more highly specialized apps. Never in the history of our species has it been so easy to be distracted. Indeed, being distracted is practically our default setting these days. But, being busy at being busy isn't a recipe for accomplishing a lot. This is what Newport is getting at in his book, and his point couldn't be more germane to the challenges we've been discussing here. Legendary consulting requires deep work, not continual distraction. Right now, as I write this, I have built myself a protective bubble against all that distraction. My phone is on airplane mode, my email account is closed, and I've zeroed my technological interface down to precisely that needed to get the work done necessary for writing this book. The technology is a fantastic tool if you make it work for you, and don't let yourself work for it. Obviously, this doesn't mean you need to be so focused and zeroed in all the time; that would be exhausting. And, indeed, as Newport observes, there is such a thing as shallow work. There's a lot of simple administrative stuff that can be done with full effectiveness while listening to your favorite podcast or music. Distinguishing between which work is deep and which is shallow is

essential to excellence in any endeavor. Once you've identified which is the deep work, create for yourself just the kind of bubble I've described to you, which I've created for myself, to write this chapter. Shut out the social media, close down all superfluous technology, zero in on what needs to be done and give it your complete attention. That's what will allow you to perform like the top one percent.

5. *Support yourself with the right tools.* As I'm sure you've noticed over the course of reading this book, I'm a huge fan of frameworks and tools. I've already shared many of these with you. I'm going to share one more, which can be really helpful. This is called the Eisenhower box. Yes, that Eisenhower: this technique was developed by Dwight D. Eisenhower, the 34th president of the United States. This box is a means for distinguishing from among those claims on your time and attention the ones that actually needed your attention and those that were just distractions.

The Eisenhower's Box

	URGENT	NOT URGENT
IMPORTANT	**DO** *Do it now* Example: Write article for today, responding to a new client request, medical issues, etc.	**DECIDE** *Schedule a time to do it* Example: Long term business strategy, exercise, calling friends and family, etc.
NO IMPORTANT	**DELEGATE** *Find someone to do it for you* Example: Scheduling meetings, booking flights, Answering certain emails, etc.	**DELETE** *Do not do it* Example: Watching television, checking social media, sorting through junk email

"What is important is seldom urgent and what is urgent is seldom important"

DWIGHT EISENHOWER

As you can see from this image, Eisenhower's Box is a two-by-two matrix. On the vertical Y axis, is a measure of "importance," while, on the horizontal X-axis, is "urgency." Items in the top left quadrant of the box are where we'll find things that are both urgent and important. These are then, of course, the items that need our immediate attention. The quadrant to the right is where we find those items that do need our attention, but not urgently. Things, like planning a long-term business strategy or taking a vacation, might be included in this corner. In the bottom left quadrant, we have items that are not important, yet are urgent. These are items that are often possible to delegate to others: travel agents, financial advisors, virtual assistants, and the like. Then, in the bottom right corner, we have items that really can be dispensed with unless there's absolutely nothing else pressing on our attention or time. When I say support yourself with tools, something like this can have a huge impact on your effectiveness. Using this tool on a daily basis, has been extremely valuable for me. You have to figure out which tools make the difference for you. And don't be shy about designing a customized tool of your own, if you recognize a need and can't find a ready solution. But always aim to utilize frameworks and tools that simplify your work, expedite your decision processes and eliminate low-value activities from your life.

6. *Build a healthy body.* It is so huge in its importance and value, it's entirely appropriate that we emphasize it as we approach the book's conclusion. Look, obviously, I'm no fitness or nutritional expert, but I know enough to assert that

within a healthy body dwells a sharp mind. It should come as no surprise that a sharp mind is an essential ingredient for producing top quality work. If our physical health suffers from neglect, the quality of our work will reflect that neglect. Eating healthily and maintaining good body weight is critically important. Likely, every reader of this book is in a different state of health. Some are more fit than others. But, from wherever you're beginning, you can take concrete actions, today, to start improving the state of your health. There is plenty of research that shows that proper nutrition and exercise sharpens the mind, aids in learning, enhances memory, improves mental stamina, enhances creativity, and lowers stress. On the nutritional side, a great introduction is Dr. Emeran Mayer's book, *The Mind-Gut Connection*. There is a massive bundle of benefits you get for the quality of your work from simply looking after yourself just as you should be doing, anyway. What better set of benefits could you ask for in your endeavor to produce high-quality work? Exercise is also important. It increases blood flow to the brain and triggers increased production of the most valuable neural chemicals: endorphins and serotonin. These chemicals help us focus while reducing our stress levels. Dr. Paul Kiell offers some profound insights into these processes (Kiell, 2010). Right nutrition and exercise establish the optimum state of your brain's operation for producing the very best quality work. Don't underestimate the value of looking good and feeling good. The self-confidence that comes with that is great and valuable, but what we're discussing here goes far beyond that. We're talking about how to hack your brain chemistry to get the absolute optimum outcome from your work effort. Every day, set aside time for physical activity and to build a healthy body. Even when you're deeply immersed in hard work, it's important to take some breaks, go for a walk, and take in some fresh air. Increased, focused, oxygen intake fuels your body and reduces your stress. All of this is key to being at the top of your game and producing top quality work.

7. *Build your own style.* This is relatively subjective. Think of this analogy. You've sat as the passenger with many drivers in your life. All of them operated within the same rules-of-the-road constraints, yet, within the boundaries of those commonly adhered to limitations; perhaps you've noticed some marked differences in how any number of them drove. Acceleration time, braking impulse, propensity to pass, curve speed, turn signal duration, even how dirty a windshield needs to be to use the wipers, and much more: all these little differences add up to what we can call the different styles of various drivers. Likewise, with consultants, we may all be aiming toward the same legendary consultant status, we may even be using the same tools in our efforts, but we all do it with our own sense of style. Think of those drivers: their styles didn't come from nowhere or overnight. It took a long time with much repetition. Hopefully, the result was a safe and responsible driving style, but whatever it was, it came with time. And the more effective it is, the more likely it is that there was conscious intent in the lessons learned while engaging in those hours logged driving. Consulting is the same: your style will come from your investment, and the time and the awareness you bring

to making that investment. There's a lot of truth in the old adage that practice makes perfect: the more consulting you do, mindfully and professionally, the higher quality you'll be able to achieve, and the more perfected your own personal style in creating that quality will become. This will enable you to differentiate yourself from everyone else in your league and resonate uniquely with your target market, resulting in repeat business.

You have your own unique experiences, which provide you with a unique story in life. High quality work, at the end of the day, is a product of your ability to marshal your story and experiences, and harness them to perform the great work which you're capable of. For these reasons, it is actually difficult to duplicate what precisely someone else is capable of doing. Your mission isn't to try to copy someone else's path to success. Rather, you want to learn the most powerful mindsets, knowledge bases, and skills from them so that you can forge your own unique path to high quality and personal success. There's nothing more you can do to provide value to your clients than to give them the very best of your own unique contributions to creating quality work.

This final chapter provided you key insights into the pillars and strategies that can allow you to produce the highest possible quality work, to provide the very highest value to your clients. Keep in mind though, such techniques are built on your ability to bring your own unique talents and disposition to the table.

Conclusion and Next Steps

*"You have brains in your head.
You have feet in your shoes.
You can steer yourself
anydirection you choose."*
- Dr. Seuss

You've now been introduced to the same system that I spent thousands of hours crafting. This legendary consulting system has the power to transform the results of your consulting efforts starting today. In fact, I would go as far as to say, even if you only implemented 50 percent of the strategies I've presented here, you would be able to position yourself as one of the top consultants in your league.

Let me leave you, with a couple of final thoughts – next steps, as it were – for you to consider. Unlocking the success available to you in this powerful consulting system, in the end, is going to boil down to two primary ideas.

First: *Raise your standards.* We all have in mind, even if only implicitly, a standard for the work we do. What do we aim for? What are we satisfied with? This is the standard which we want to meet in our lives. We all have an internalized image of who we are and what we're capable of. Let me use a monetary standard, only because the quantified character of the example makes it a graphic illustration. Every individual has in mind a dollar figure that represents what they believe they're capable of earning. That range can stretch from practically nothing to the absolute heights of conceivable financial success. Those with astronomical aspirations may initially strike you as unrealistic: only a tiny fraction of the world population makes that kind of money. On the other hand, people with such a peak upper limit to their imagined monetary capacity have not set limits on themselves that hold them down. They may not, in the end, get rich. But if they fail to do so, it wasn't because they set for themselves limitations that ruled out possibilities from the start.

The same thing applies to your relationship with work. We all have a preconceived standard of what we can achieve. Legendary consultants do not get to be a part of the top one percent by assuming they were capable only of producing pedestrian work. Don't let your own preconception of possibility set a limit on your potential. My invitation to you is to raise your standards. No amount of information, no set of skills, no strategy, will enable you to do great work if you fail to set greatness as your goal.

Simply refuse to allow yourself to do work that is less than legendary.

It is always our initial intention that propels us in the direction of our eventual outcome. Be sure that your initial intention is always to be legendary. Consciously, deliberately, raise your standards, at all times. Only then will you be confident that your initial intentions are always aiming you in the direction of legendary consulting.

Second: This idea that I want to leave you with is a lesson that I learned from my grandmother. This was a life-changing lesson for me and can be one for you, too. It can allow you achieve so much more value out of your work and life. It is indeed a key that can unlock the tremendous potential inherent in this legendary consulting system, which I've shared with you in this book. To fully understand this lesson, let me take you back to the most challenging time of my life. This was when I moved to Canada. I've already shared with you stories about the difficulties I faced then. I felt lonely, incompetent, and unworthy. I was convinced at times that I was doomed to be a failure. I was frustrated and felt emotionally depleted. I was very close to moving back home to India and abandoning my dream of building a career out of North America.

It was in the midst of all this that I had a conversation with my grandmother. I told her, grandma, life is very difficult here in Canada. Perhaps I should move back to India and try to do something there. Her reply, I remember was: Son, everything new is difficult, at first. You're in a new country, in a new culture, amongst new people. It is bound to be difficult. But that doesn't mean it will always stay difficult. If you stick to your dream, if you keep moving toward your goals, with time, it will get easy. Be true to who you are and stand by your principles, one day it will all seem easy. *If you stick, it will click.*

Now, obviously, my grandmother said this to me in Hindi. I've translated it for you and offered this mnemonic rhyme – if you stick, it will click.

And my grandmother was exactly right. It turned out just as she said it would. Once I stuck it out, through those hard times, eventually, it did get much easier. That perseverance is responsible for the options I have open to me today. Honestly, it's a little disconcerting, even scary, to think how things might have turned out if I had not followed my grandmother's wise advice and not stuck to my goals and values.

I offer this little story from my life to you in the hope it will inspire you to move forward toward your dreams. It won't always be easy, trying to implement these many skills, frameworks, strategies, and mindsets that I offer, here. There will be times you'll feel overwhelmed. Maybe you'll even experience something like the frustration and discouragement I experienced at that time. If you do, please remember what she said, everything new is difficult at first but that does not mean it will always stay difficult. Persevere. If you stick to it; it will get easier. *If you stick, it will click.*

I invite you to keep this pearl of wisdom from my grandmother in mind, not only in learning and implementing the lessons of this book, but as a beacon by which to live your life. Life is a series of unending challenges. The life we create is built on our response to those series of challenges. Often it feels easier to give up and metaphorically go home. However, you can overcome those challenges. Every single one that life throws your way. And, it isn't ever easy at first. But, it always gets easier, if you stick to your guns. If you stick, eventually, it will click. Each time. In all life's challenges.

An important aspect of sticking, and sticking effectively, is making sure you have a plan for moving forward. The lessons in this book will most effectively help you if you take these lessons and mold them into a plan – for your business and for your life. Think of it as a standard operating procedure. How will you operate moving forward? Which values and standards will inform your choices and how will you implement those choices? This is a point which has been continually reiterated throughout the book and, as we come to its end, that point needs to be said once more: nothing great, nothing legendary, has ever been achieved without rigorous, robust planning. As true as that is for any specific consulting project, it is also true of how you run your

Conclusion and Next Steps

consulting business. Indeed, it is true of how you live your life.

I invite you to use the ideas, the insights, and the strategies in this book to think through your life plan. How are you going to live your life? How are you going to achieve legendary consulting status? This book is a powerful tool for cutting through life's underbrush. Only you can determine which exact path needs to be cleared. The discussion at the start of the book will help. Determine what your core values are, your vision for your own life? Then, how do you implement it? What time will you get up to start your day? With what food will you fuel your body? Are you going to ensure you have the physical exercise necessary to maintain a strong, nimble mind? That foundation allows you to take a determined step forward in molding your business. What kind of a consultant will you be? How will you approach new business challenges? How will you build relationships with your clients? Each more precise step grows organically out of the strong foundation for living your life.

I urge you, after you've completed this book, to sit with yourself for three or four hours. Reflect on what you've read in this book. Possibly, skim through it, reviewing your own comments as you read. Try to absorb it as thoroughly as you're able, then take that step to start building yourself a plan, and remember, if you stick, it will click.

It has been an honor for me to serve you, through this book. I invite you to reach for those legendary standards that will give you the life you desire. Commit to doing legendary work and living a legendary life. I hope someday we have the opportunity to meet in person. Please share with me the breakthroughs you've achieved with the help of this book.

My email address is

me@himanshunarang.com

I would be thrilled and honored if you share with me the stories of how this book, I modestly offer you, has helped you strive toward your goals of legendary consulting.

Thank you.

Readings

Alexander, R. D. (1974). The Evolution of Social Behavior. Annual Review of Ecology and Systematics, 5, 325–383.

Alexander, R. D. (1982). *Darwinism and Human Affairs*. Seattle: University of Washington Press.

Awamleh, R., & Gardner, W. L. (1999). Perceptions of leader charisma and effectiveness: The effects of vision content, delivery, and organizational performance. *The Leadership Quarterly, 10*(3), 345–373. https://doi.org/10.1016/S1048-9843(99)00022-3

Bailey, C. (2016). *The Productivity Project: Accomplishing More by Managing Your Time, Attention, and Energy*. New York: Random House Canada.

Bowles, D., & Cooper, C. (2009). *Employee Morale: Driving Performance in Challenging Times* (2009 edition). Houndmills, Basingstoke, Hampshire ; New York: Palgrave Macmillan.

Burka, J. B., & Yuen, L. M. (2008). *Procrastination: Why You Do It, What to Do About It Now* (2 edition). Cambridge, MA: Da Capo Lifelong Books.

Cosmides, L., Tooby, J., Fiddick, L., & Bryant, G. A. (2005). Detecting cheaters. *Trends in Cognitive Sciences, 9*(10.1016/j.tics.2005.09.005), 505–506. https://doi.org/http://dx.doi.org/10.1016/j.tics.2005.09.005

Csikszentmihalyi, M. (2008). *Flow: The Psychology of Optimal Experience* (1 edition). New York: Harper Perennial Modern Classics.

Defensive Body Language. (n.d.). Retrieved June 27, 2017, from http://www.study-body-language.com/Defensive-body-language.html

Donahue, H. W. (Ed.). (2010). *The Toastmaster's Manual*. Kessinger Publishing, LLC.

Eagleman, D. M. (2008). Human time perception and its illusions. *Current Opinion in Neurobiology, 18*(2), 131–136. https://doi.org/10.1016/j.conb.2008.06.002

Emmons, R. (2008). *Thanks!: How Practicing Gratitude Can Make You Happier* (Reprint edition). New York: Mariner Books.

Fahmy, S. (2008, February 28). Low-intensity exercise reduces fatigue symptoms by 65 percent, study finds | University of Georgia Today. Retrieved April 28, 2017, from http://news.uga.edu/releases/article/low-intensity-exercise-reduces-fatigue-symptoms-by-65-percent-study-finds/

Ferrari, B. T. (2012). *Power Listening: Mastering the Most Critical Business Skill of All*. New York: Portfolio.

Goudreau, J. (2012, November 30). The Seven Ways Your Boss Is Judging Your Appearance | Forbes. Retrieved April 28, 2017, from http://www.forbes.com/sites/jennagoudreau/2012/11/30/the-seven-ways-your-boss-is-judging-your-appearance/

Groth, A. (2012). Jim Rohn: You're The Average Of The Five People You Spend The Most Time With | Business Insider. Retrieved June 29, 2017, from http://www.businessinsider.com/jim-rohn-youre-the-average-of-the-five-people-you-spend-the-most-time-with-2012-7

Gleicher, D. (1960). : Formula for Change | Wikipedia. Retrieved Feb 16, 2018, from https://en.wikipedia.org/wiki/Formula_for_change

Haidt, J. (2012). *The Righteous Mind: Why Good People Are Divided by Politics and Religion* (1 edition). Vintage.

Hedges, K. (2014, November 14). Six Ways To Avoid Death By PowerPoint | Forbes. Retrieved June 27, 2017, from http://www.forbes.com/sites/work-in-progress/2014/11/14/six-ways-to-avoid-death-by-powerpoint/

Hillman, C. H., Erickson, K. I., & Kramer, A. F. (2008). Be smart, exercise your heart: exercise effects on brain and cognition. *Nature Reviews Neuroscience*, 9(1), 58–65. https://doi.org/10.1038/nrn2298

Iacoboni, M. (2009). *Mirroring People: The Science of Empathy and How We Connect with Others* (Original edition). New York: Picador.

Kahan, D. M. (2013). *Ideology, Motivated Reasoning, and Cognitive Reflection: An Experimental Study* (SSRN Scholarly Paper No. ID 2182588). Rochester, NY: Social Science Research Network. Retrieved from http://papers.ssrn.com/abstract=2182588

Kahan, D. M., Peters, E., Wittlin, M., Slovic, P., Ouellette, L. L., Braman, D., & Mandel, G. (2012). The polarizing impact of science literacy and numeracy on perceived climate change risks. *Nature Climate Change*, 2(10), 732–735. https://doi.org/10.1038/nclimate1547

Kahneman, D. (2013). *Thinking, Fast and Slow* (1st edition). New York: Farrar, Straus and Giroux.

Kern, H. (2014). *Going from Undisciplined to Self Mastery: Five Simple Steps to Get You There*. Virginia Beach, VA: Koehler Books.

Kiell, P. J. (2010). *Exercise and the Mind: The Possibilities for Mind-Body-Spirit Unity*. Halcottsville, NY: Breakaway Books.

Kotter, J. P. (2002). *Leading Change*. Boston: Harvard Business Review Press.

Lubin, G., & Gillett, R. (2016). 21 successful people who wake up incredibly early | Business Insider. Retrieved June 29, 2017, from http://www.businessinsider.com/successful-people-who-wake-up-really-early-2016-4

Lyberg, L. E., Biemer, P. P., Collins, M., Leeuw, E. de, Dippo, C., Schwarz, N., & Trewin, D. (Eds.). (1997). *Survey Measurement and Process Quality* (1 edition). New York: Wiley-Interscience.

Mayer, E. (2016). *The Mind-Gut Connection: How the Hidden Conversation Within Our Bodies Impacts Our Mood, Our Choices, and Our Overall Health*. New York, NY: Harper Wave.

Mehrabian, A. (1972). *Silent Messages: Implicit Communication of Emotions and Attitudes*. Belmont, Calif: Wadsworth Publishing Company.

Mikulincer, M., & Shaver, P. R. (Eds.). (2010). *Prosocial motives, emotions, and behavior: The better angels of our nature*. Washington, DC, US: American Psychological Association. https://doi.org/10.1037/12061-012

Navarro, J. (2012). *The Power of Body Language* (Abridged edition). Simon & Schuster Audio/Nightingale-Conant.

Newport, C. (2016). *Deep Work: Rules for Focused Success in a Distracted World*. Grand Central Publishing.

O'Neal, G. S., & Lapitsky, M. (1991). Effects of Clothing as Nonverbal Communication on Credibility of the Message Source. *Clothing and Textiles Research Journal, 9*(3), 28–34. https://doi.org/10.1177/0887302X9100900305

Paul, A. M. (2013, March 18). Four Ways to Give Good Feedback. *Time*. Retrieved from http://ideas.time.com/2013/03/18/four-ways-to-give-good-feedback/

Pozen, R. C. (2001, November 30). Exercise Increases Productivity | Brookings Institution. Retrieved April 28, 2017, from https://www.brookings.edu/opinions/exercise-increases-productivity/

Pozen, R. C. (2013, March 28). The Delicate Art of Giving Feedback | Harvard Business Review. Retrieved June 27, 2017, from https://hbr.org/2013/03/the-delicate-art-of-giving-fee

Robbins, N. (2012, November 20). Public Speaking Mistakes to Avoid | Forbes. Retrieved June 27, 2017, from http://www.forbes.com/sites/naomirobbins/2012/11/20/public-speaking-mistakes-to-avoid/

Robbins, T. (2014, December 4). Tony Robbins: 6 Basic Needs That Make Us Tick | Entrepreneur. Retrieved March 9, 2017, from https://www.entrepreneur.com/article/240441

Sant, T. (2003). *Persuasive Business Proposals: Writing to Win More Customers, Clients, and Contracts* (2 edition). New York: AMACOM Books.

Saunders, E. G. (2015). Do You Really Need to Hold That Meeting? | Harvard Business Review. Retrieved June 27, 2017, from https://hbr.org/2015/03/do-you-really-need-to-hold-that-meeting

Sgroi, D. (2015, October 27). Happiness and productivity: Understanding the happy-productive worker | Social Market Foundation. Retrieved April 28, 2017, from http://www.smf.co.uk/publications/happiness-and-productivity-understanding-the-happy-productive-worker/

Shandrow, K. L. (2014, October). How to Dress for a Business Meeting. Yes, Seriously. (Infographic) | Entrepreneur. Retrieved June 27, 2017, from https://www.entrepreneur.com/article/238953

Smith, D. L. (2007). *Why We Lie: The Evolutionary Roots of Deception and the Unconscious Mind*. St. Martin's Griffin.

Sugiyama, M. S. (1996). On the origins of narrative. *Human Nature*, *7*(4), 403–425. https://doi.org/10.1007/BF02732901

Tomporowski, P. D. (2003). Effects of acute bouts of exercise on cognition. *Acta Psychologica*, *112*(3), 297–324.

Trivers, R. (2014). *The Folly of Fools: The Logic of Deceit and Self-Deception in Human Life* (First Trade Paper Edition edition). Basic Books.

Troiani, M. V., & Mercer, M. W. (1998). *Spontaneous Optimism: Proven Strategies for Health, Prosperity & Happiness*. Lake Zurich, Ill.: Castlegate Publishers, Inc.

Tversky, A., & Kahneman, D. (1974). Judgment under Uncertainty: Heuristics and Biases. *Science*, *185*(4157), 1124–1131. https://doi.org/10.1126/science.185.4157.1124

UCL. (2009, August 4). How long does it take to form a habit? Retrieved April 28, 2017, from https://www.ucl.ac.uk/news/news-articles/0908/09080401

Vaden, R. (2015). *Procrastinate on Purpose: 5 Permissions to Multiply Your Time* (Reprint edition). TarcherPerigee.

Vohs, K. D., & Baumeister, R. F. (Eds.). (2016). *Handbook of Self-Regulation, Third Edition: Research, Theory, and Applications* (3 edition). New York: The Guilford Press.

BEX

Made in the USA
Columbia, SC
17 April 2018